WOMEN SET FREE

Also by Wendy Virgo
LEADING LADIES

Women
Set Free

WENDY VIRGO

KINGSWAY PUBLICATIONS
EASTBOURNE

Copyright © Wendy Virgo 1989

First published 1989

All rights reserved.
No part of this publication may be reproduced or
transmitted in any form or by any means, electronic
or mechanical, including photocopy, recording, or any
information storage and retrieval system, without
permission in writing from the publisher.

Biblical quotations are from the
New American Standard Bible © The Lockman Foundation
1960, 1962, 1963, 1968, 1971, 1972, 1973

Front cover design by Vic Mitchell

British Library Cataloguing in Publication Data

Virgo, Wendy
  Women set free.
  1. Women. Christian life
  I. Title
  248.8'43

ISBN 0-86065-767-1

Printed in Great Britain for
KINGSWAY PUBLICATIONS LTD
1 St Anne's Road, Eastbourne, E Sussex BN21 3UN by
Richard Clay Ltd, Bungay, Suffolk.
Typeset by Nuprint Ltd, Harpenden, Herts AL5 4SE

Contents

1. Freedom Starts Here — 7
2. Freedom from Condemnation — 15
3. Freedom from Bondage — 28
4. Freedom from Unbelief — 42
5. Freedom from Frustration — 52
6. Freedom from Bitterness — 63
7. Freedom and Identity — 77
8. Freedom to be Whole-hearted — 92
9. Freedom to Forgive — 101
10. Freedom and Authority — 114
11. Freedom and the Will of God — 132
12. Using Truth to Fight for Freedom — 150
13. The Vision of Freedom — 155

*To my darling daughter Anna.
May she ever enjoy God's freedom.*

1

Freedom Starts Here

It was a Whit Sunday afternoon in May. Through the open window floated warm, summer sounds: bees buzzing, the knock of bats against balls and the laughter of children. As I sat on the wooden bench in its patch of sunlight, I felt pleasantly warm and happy—if somewhat jammed between other jostling youngsters who met each Sunday in a Bible class known as Crusaders.

I had grown used to coming to this class at weekends. It was part of the routine of my childhood. As firmly committed Christians, my parents had woven their faith in God into our family life. We belonged to a Brethren Assembly where teaching for children was rather limited, so when my parents met the couple who ran two flourishing Crusader groups in the town, one for boys and one for girls, they decided to send their four daughters to the girls' class.

My childhood days were a happy jumble of bonfires in the back garden, roller-skating on the quiet roads around our house, keeping chickens, planting runner beans and picking apples and blackberries. I remember sunlit evening strolls along the narrow path by the railway cutting. We always called it the 'rabbit path' because on summer evenings, scores of rabbits would be scampering and playing in the field opposite.

Ours was not a lavish home in a material sense. Indeed, there was never a lot of money around. But we had plenty of fresh vegetables and fruit from the garden, new laid eggs, an abundance of fun and fresh air, and freedom to enjoy it. It was, for us children at any rate, a pretty carefree existence.

I was privileged to grow up in a post-war era, so I knew nothing of the tension and fear generated by being a nation at war. It was also an era before the moral abandonment and excesses of the sixties. Perhaps our memories are viewed through rose-tinted spectacles, but I seem to remember a time when murder was a rarity, when the news of such a crime brought a chill of horror and when people talked about it in shocked whispers. It was possible then for two or three twelve-year-old girls to pack their lunch and an old frying pan and cycle up into the hills where they could make a fire and stay all day without anyone worrying about them. It was a time when teachers were called 'Sir' and old ladies were respected and visited with bunches of flowers and, at Christmas, tins of humbugs. If a little girl broke her sandal strap while she was running an errand for her mother, she could pop into the cobbler's shop and he would stitch it up, there and then, for nothing.

Of course, it wasn't all idyllic. Inevitably, in a family where four girls were born close together, there were scraps and quarrels. It was often noisy and boisterous and my mother must have been driven to distraction by our untidiness and fierce arguments. But on the whole, they were storms that arose suddenly and subsided quickly. Stinging palms and bottoms bore testimony to discipline that was swift and thorough.

Thankfully, I never had to bear the horrors of coldness or hostility between my parents. We children lived unthreatened by the spectre of separation or divorce. I am sure that the possibility of such things happening never entered our heads. We believed we belonged to a normal family and I naïvely assumed that our experience was normal for other families too.

So there it was: a healthy, carefree life; full of love, fun, security, simplicity and solid values. It was free in the main from anxiety, and free from fears of all sorts. So why does that Whit Sunday in May stand out? Why was it so significant?

I had much that many people would yearn for. What more did I need? I had health, strength, love, security and family life. Surely the basics were all there? Surely I had the potential for growing up into a confident, unwarped human being who would find an excellent place in society?

These things, although undoubtedly important factors in developing my personality and outlook, were not enough on their own. On that Sunday in 1953, something happened that was nothing less than dynamic, the repercussions of which still continue to reverberate through my life.

Usually at the Crusader class, there was a short time of singing and prayer before the girls divided into several groups for teaching according to age. However, on this particular day we all stayed together and

Mrs Green, the leader, addressed us all. Whenever she spoke, there was never any fidgeting or yawning, and this day was no exception. Since it was Whit Sunday, she probably wanted to talk to us about the first Pentecost and the Holy Spirit. I cannot remember anything she said, but she held our attention until the end. That is where the mists of time clear and I can recall the events which followed with startling clarity. In order to underline and illustrate some points in her talk, she began to read a poem.

It was a somewhat solemn poem. My attention was riveted to its story, about a man who repeatedly heard the voice of God calling him at intervals through his life. First, the Holy Spirit challenged him as a young boy to make Jesus Christ the captain of his life, but he did not respond. Again, the Spirit called him in his teen years and again in his twenties and thirties and so on throughout his life. But the man hardened his heart. Eventually, on his death-bed, God gave him the opportunity once more to receive mercy, but even at the last moment, the man chose not to yield. There was an awesome stillness in the room as Mrs Green read the final line: 'And turning over on his pillow, he died.'

I knew the man had slipped into eternity without God. The Spirit would not come to him any more. He was now in darkness for ever. Mrs Green simply explained that at this very moment, we could choose to receive what that man had refused: the love and forgiveness of God. I heard that same voice calling me. I knew I wanted to respond. I wanted to seize the opportunity. I wanted to know that when I died I would go to heaven. I didn't want to die without God and I didn't want to live without him either. There, on that wooden bench with fast beating heart, I shut my eyes and bowed my head, 'Lord, Jesus, please come into my life, wash me clean inside. I give my life to you.' No deep grasp of theology, just a simple, childish prayer.

Something happened. God came! The explosion of joy inside told me that he had heard. The room was sunny before; now it was sunnier. I was happy before; now I was happier. Everything seemed new, but it was I who was new and I would never be the same again.

The person sitting next to me was totally unaware that anything had happened, but within me such a profound change had taken place that it seemed as if my previous light was darkness. At the tender age of seven, I had entered a freedom which I progressively appreciated as the years went by.

People yearn for freedom. It has been the cry of many hearts through the centuries. Freedom from oppression and tyranny; from pain and sickness, poverty, degradation, fear and worry. It is the subject of songs, the reason for protest marches, the motivation for assassinations, coups and conflicts. The desire for it has vented itself in anger and violence or sometimes in passivity and inertia. In their search for freedom, some people precipitate action by taking the law into their own hands, while others do the opposite and drop out. In rejecting society with its current codes and values, they seek to establish an individual separation that is not dependent on, or obligated to, anyone. So how can I say that a little girl of seven can find the key when so many others are still blindly groping for the door?

Man is right in his desire to be free, but he continually fails to understand the fundamental nature of his captivity. Yes, he is enslaved, but by what and by whom? As he struggles to shake off external shackles, he neglects the most basic problem of all: the bondage of the human heart.

This captivity is no respecter of persons. Every human being carries within himself the seeds of his own destruction. His attitudes and appetites are fundamentally self-orientated and anti-God. He is biased towards the bad, and although outwardly he may improve himself or his surroundings, his efforts are superficial. They are insufficient for permanent peace because the roots of his nature remain untouched. He will always sink back into his natural slime, as if a lead weight were exerting a gravitational pull on his soul.

How can he cut himself free from this weight and float upwards? He can't. Man is a tragic figure, a majestic ruin. He was made in the image of God and retains some of the splendour to which he is heir. He also confesses occasionally to aspirations after goodness and purity, but he is unable to attain the spiritual or moral heights to which he aspires. The harder he tries to climb, the more disillusioned he becomes with himself and with the rest of the world. He makes rules for himself but becomes further entangled in the bondage of having to keep them. So he abandons rules and becomes bogged down in the inevitable morass that results when there are no guidelines.

'Who can deliver me?' cried the apostle Paul in despair. His words have found a place in the mouths of both good people and criminals since the Garden of Eden.

Freedom must begin on the inside. It must start with the discovery of peace with God. That tendency to rebel has to be terminated and a new focus found which is directed away from the self and which finds in God both its source and its end.

FREEDOM STARTS HERE

It begins in the recognition that only God in Jesus Christ can change the human heart. When Jesus lived as a man, he identified with humanity in every way. He was a man but without that fundamental flaw that makes other men sin. When he died, he laid down his perfect life as a sacrifice to God on our behalf. He paid the ultimate price to release us from sin and death. God saw his Son hanging in a broken, bloody mess on the cross and shouted through the heavens, 'It is enough! Jesus has paid dearly for man's sin and I receive his sacrifice. For his sake, I will have mercy. They are accepted in the Beloved.'

The price has been paid for our freedom. The lock on the cage has been broken, but we can remain in our cage and try to fight our way out by battering at all the other bars. Jesus said, 'I am the door.' He is the only way to true, lasting freedom.

Freedom begins here—not with grandiose schemes, ideological reforms, attempts to be better, social change or revolution. Those all have their place, but later down the line. Change must begin in the human heart which humbles itself as it stands before that narrow door. The door is too narrow to admit pride, intellectualism, prestige, or trappings of wealth, celebrity or personal prowess. They must be dumped outside. The human heart must stand there, painfully stripped bare, naked. 'But if any man enter in, he shall be saved and shall go in and out and find pasture.'

God doesn't want you plus what you have accumulated. Your accumulations are obstructions to freedom. He wants you on your own. As you put out a hand to push the door, though it looks unbelievably narrow, even insignificant, you find that it swings open onto vistas unimagined. You forget about what you left behind. Those things now seem so tawdry and shabby. How could you have thought them so important? Your nakedness is forgotten as you receive new garments of righteousness, love and acceptance. Now begins the real adventure as you explore the implications of this freedom. You are free from the burden of guilt which fell off as you passed through the door. Now you will find as you travel on that this freedom is wider than you first realised. You are in a new dimension where, in Jesus, there is freedom from fear, bitterness, anxiety, anger, self-pity and many other enemies. These things will still try to trap you and bind you up, but where the Spirit of the Lord is, there is liberty.

2

Freedom from Condemnation

The sun was well risen. A shaft of light penetrated the small, high window and flickered on the cheek of the woman on the bed. She stirred and blinked her sleepy eyes and stared uncertainly around the shadowy, unfamiliar room. The memories returned. Languidly, she turned over and stretched a hand out to the other side of the bed.

Her lover was already awake. There was anxiety in his eyes. 'It's late,' he murmured. Sounds of day floated through the window. 'This is a noisy street,' she thought, and was about to say so when her lover forestalled her. 'What's all that shouting about?' he said abruptly. At the same moment, there came a hammering on the door and the indistinct shouts became a babble of angry words and accusations.

Panic-stricken, the couple gazed at each other.

'What shall we do?' she whispered.

'Escape!' he replied.

As quickly as the word left his lips he was out of the bed, into a robe and out of the room by a back way. Seconds later, the door to the main hallway crashed open and an excited mob filled the chamber where she, petrified, was still lying.

'There she is! Caught in his bed! Where is he? Can't be far away. The sheets are still warm.' She cowered before their accusing eyes, trying to cover herself with the bedclothes. She could not look up and meet their eyes, but she knew that they would be filled with contempt and triumph. Contempt in the eyes of those who had always regarded her as a slut and were now simply confirming their suspicions. Triumph in the eyes of those who didn't care for her or her husband, but who wanted a victim who had fallen foul of the law.

She knew it would be useless to argue. There she was—in his bed! It was fruitless to plead that she was young; that her husband was old. It was futile to plead for mercy. The law was unrelenting in its condemnation. There was no loophole; she could not plead mitigating circumstances. She was guilty, guilty, guilty! She knew her fate—death by stoning.

They dragged her, shaking with terror, like a captured animal, out onto the street. As they swept her along, they were joined by others who, scenting blood, swelled the small crowd into an excited mob. It was not every day that the revered Pharisees were seen striding along with stern expressions and tassels swinging, followed by a noisy rabble who pushed and jostled a dishevelled, half-naked young woman towards the Temple. But it was not unknown either. She would be taken before the doctors of the law and if pronounced guilty, she would be dragged outside

FREEDOM FROM CONDEMNATION

the city to a large pit where stones and boulders would be thrown at her until she died. It was a violent, horrifying death, unpredictably short or long, depending on the accuracy of the throwers.

There was nothing she could do. Dust, noise, rough hands, shame, humiliation, guilt and fear combined into a nightmare. Twist and turn as she may, there was no way out of those imprisoning hands—just as there was no way out of the guilt that lay heavily in her soul.

If only she had turned away the moment his eyes had met hers! If only she had not responded to those signals of attraction with alluring signals of her own. If only she had not allowed his hand to linger on hers; not allowed whispered confidences and caresses; not allowed the chemistry to keep fizzing when a few well-chosen words could have dampened it down. If only she had not told him that her husband was away on business. If only....

But she had gone along with the game—a willing conspirator—enjoying the flattery, the intrigue, the intimate secrets. She had known all along that they were taking risks. But somehow in the heady haze of romance, the likelihood of being caught had seemed distant and unreal. 'Surely it couldn't happen to us?'

And so, like hundreds before and since, she had made her decision. She had played with fire and now she was about to burn. What had started out as a harmless bit of fun had turned into something rather more serious. Adultery, said the law, was sin. Adultery was punishable by death.

There was no arguing with the law. It was always right. It pointed out your sin, but didn't stop you doing it. It exposed it for what it was, but knew nothing of tenderness. It never allowed for human feelings like: 'If you're in love, it's all right,' or, 'You need to find self-awareness by doing your own thing,' or, 'If you can't be good, be careful.' Oh no! The law was razor-sharp, clear and uncompromising. It pulled your actions out of the soft, blurred shadows of the bedroom and hung them out in the glare of the noonday sun where they were exposed unequivocally as sin. Then it pronounced the sinner 'Guilty!'—and there was no escape.

They reached the Temple and entered one of the outer courts. The scribes and Pharisees seemed to know exactly where to go. Unhesitatingly, they made for a corner where a small group of people were gathered around a rabbi. One of the Pharisees grabbed the woman by the arm and thrust her forward. She fell awkwardly in the middle of the circle of men—at the feet of the seated teacher. The rest of her accusers pressed around. The spokesman, with the air of importance that one assumes when he feels himself to be in an unassailable position, announced, 'Teacher, we have caught this woman in the act of adultery. Now, in the law, Moses commanded us to stone such women. What do you say?'

There was silence. The crowd was hushed, dimly aware that more was at stake than the life of this sinful woman. The lawyers and Pharisees watched him narrowly. They knew they were playing a trump card. Would Jesus of Nazareth, whom some proclaimed the Messiah, bow to the law? Would he acknowledge its supremacy and admit that he was unable to change a jot or tittle? Or would he set it aside on grounds of compassion and lay himself open to the charge of being a law-breaker and a rebel?

Jesus bent forward and doodled in the sand with his finger. Only the woman could see his face. She did not know then that she stood between law and grace, Moses and Jesus. On one side the law, undeniably right and righteous, accused and condemned her. On the other, the Son of God, also undeniably right and righteous. Would he also accuse and condemn?

The Pharisees added to the accusations and pressed for an answer but Jesus continued to draw in the dust. Curiously, she watched him. He was in no hurry. He was not yielding to pressure. In fact, he seemed quite composed. She got the distinct impression that he was waiting, listening for an answer. The more he delayed, the more heated they grew in their allegations. Suddenly, Jesus stood up and calmly looked around the crowd. The clamour ceased and he quietly but distinctly delivered his counsel. 'He who is without sin among you, let him be the first to throw a stone at her.' Then he sat down again and resumed his doodling in the dust.

Some faces flushed with consternation, frustration and suppressed rage, while others were drained of their aggressive, indignant appearance. What were the implications of Jesus' comment? The older and wiser men were the first to turn and walk away. They recognised that they were not without sin. The younger ones, full of righteous indignation and arrogance, were less inclined to drop their stones. But they too eventually melted away.

The woman, who a few minutes earlier had been about to die, suddenly encountered an immovable rock—the grace of God. That morning, she had anticipated a terrifying, agonising and totally deserved death. Now, looking into the face of Jesus Christ, she was confronted with grace and truth. Could she possibly be about to receive a verdict which was absolutely undeserved?

His eyes met her incredulous gaze. 'Does no one condemn you?' he asked her gently. 'No one, Lord,' she said. 'Neither do I condemn you,' he replied. 'Go your way. Do not sin any more.'

As he said this, a great weight seemed to fall off her. She was free. There was no more condemnation; she had been reprieved; she was no longer under sentence of death. There was no more guilt either. She had sinned and the law had exposed her sin and brought her to Christ. He had declared, 'No condemnation.' He did not require her to work off her guilt; to try and atone for it; to do penitential deeds; to pay a fne or go to prison. There was nothing to pay.

'Do not sin any more,' he had said. At last, she had the power over sin! She could go and live out her freedom. She did not have to suffer under the weight of her sinfulness any more. She did not have to live under the law—indeed, if she tried to do this, she would be powerless to live a sinless life. The law could only define, expose and condemn sin. It could not empower. 'For what the Law could not do, weak as it was through the flesh, God did: sending His own Son...as an offering for sin, He condemned sin in the flesh' (Rom 8:3). Once the 'law of the Spirit of life in Christ Jesus' has taken over, it has 'set you free from the law of sin and death' (Rom 8:2). This woman was no longer forced to live under the heavy yoke of the law. She could, instead, obey Jesus out of a totally different motivation—love.

Jesus was saying to her what Paul would later write to the Roman Christians: 'Do not go on presenting the members of your body to sin as instruments of unrighteousness; but present yourselves to God as those alive from the dead, and your members as instruments of righteousness to God' (Rom 6:13).

Go and do not sin. It sounds so simple but it is at this point that many Christians get stuck. Me included!

It was during my late teens—and following a period of backsliding—that I began to read the book of Romans. I was particularly thrilled by chapter 5 which was instrumental in turning me back to God. Needless to say, it felt wonderful to know again the grace and peace of God. I was reminded that God had taken the initiative by sending his Son to die in my place. His love for me was overwhelming, his forgiveness free and undeserved.

I read on, into chapter 6: 'Consider yourselves to be dead to sin, but alive to God'; 'Do not let sin reign in your mortal body'; 'Sin shall not be master over you.'

These statements puzzled me. Especially the bit about sin not being master over me. The way I understood that was, 'You won't sin now because you are a Christian.' The trouble was that I did sin!

It was difficult at school. I fell into using bad language and allowed my temper to get the better of me. I made cutting remarks and failed to do my homework assignments. The Christian life was clearly an uphill struggle and in no way did I seem to be any different from my school mates! I felt confused and resentful and I remember arguing with the church youth leader at the bus-stop one evening. 'It says sin shall not be master over you, but it jolly well *is*!' I exploded. 'Am I saved or not? Why isn't the Bible true for *me*? I always seem to be doing wrong things.'

Patiently he tried to clarify the Scriptures for me, but I couldn't grasp it. To my way of thinking, I was living a contradiction—a forgiven sinner who still sinned!

My solution to this was to tell myself, 'You must

just try harder; concentrate on trying to be a good girl; do all the things a Christian should do and don't do the things a Christian shouldn't!' So I tried—not very successfully—to adhere to a self-imposed set of rules.

'I must get up early and pray.' I failed here. I got up early enough, but it was to do a paper-round, not pray!

'I will not wear make-up.' This became diluted to, '...except at weekends or at parties.'

'I will not have boyfriends.' This became amended to, '...until the next nice looking boy comes along.'

I struggled like this for years. I wanted to please God. I wanted to live a holy life. But I imposed rules upon myself in order to achieve my goal—then I despised myself when I failed to keep them. There was a period while I was at Bible College, when, instead of eating lunch on a Sunday, I would go to my room and pray. It wasn't long before I was cutting out breakfast and tea as well. Then I began to include Saturday fasting and finally fasted for the whole weekend.

Now, fasting in its place is fruitful and beneficial, but when it is a self-imposed ritual which is undertaken to boost up one's spiritual ego, all it produces is pride. I began to suspect something was wrong when I realised I was in danger of looking down on those who were doing something as worldly as enjoy Sunday lunch!

Light began to dawn when I was baptised in the Holy Spirit. I fell in love with Jesus all over again. Indeed, I was so busy enjoying his love and companionship, I didn't think too much about sin, and some of my rules no longer seemed important—or even right!

Nevertheless, there were times when I did wrong things and afterwards I felt very bad indeed. One

FREEDOM FROM CONDEMNATION

occasion is sharp in my memory. By this time I was engaged to Terry. He was still at Bible College, but I was working in the East End of London. We had limited opportunities to be together, so when one of my friends offered to let me stay at her flat near the college while she was away for the weekend, I took the opportunity and borrowed her front door key.

Her flat was on the ground floor of a house which was owned by an old lady. Very late on the Saturday night, I let myself into the house and went to sleep on the bed downstairs. I was awakened early the next morning, by a poker-waving, irate old lady in a hairnet and dressing-gown! It turned out that between us, my friend and I had neglected to inform this poor old lady that I would be using the flat in her absence. When, at midnight, she heard the key turning in the lock and realised that someone was stealthily moving around downstairs, she was terrified out of her wits. She had been unable to sleep all night and when she eventually discovered that I was the culprit she was understandably furious.

I left her house feeling subdued, chastened and horribly guilty for causing such distress. It was Sunday morning, so I met Terry and we went to church.

I could not enter into worship. I was so overcome by condemnation. I could not lift up my head, let alone my hands! Every time I attempted to join in, the arrows of condemnation would stab me. 'How can you possibly worship God after putting that old woman through that ordeal? You're thoughtless, heartless and inconsiderate! How could God receive worship from you? You're a thorough hypocrite! Your praise is just pretence!' I was in thorough agreement with all this and sat in miserable silence for the entire morning.

After the meeting, Terry and I headed for the nearest underground railway station. We stood waiting for a train and discussed the situation. 'Your trouble is, you're still trying to earn God's love by keeping laws,' he said. 'So when you break one of your laws you think he's stopped loving you and you've got to earn his love all over again. But Jesus' love for you hasn't changed because of what happened to that old lady. You could do it again tonight and he would still love you!' I was aghast. This was practically blasphemy!

'Look,' he said patiently, 'I love you because you're you, not because you're trying to earn my love. I would still love you if you lay in bed all day and did nothing! Now Jesus' love is like that, only much, much greater. You don't have to do anything to make him love you. He loves you anyway!'

'Are you sure?' I gasped.

'Absolutely,' he insisted. 'That also means that there is nothing you can do that will make him stop loving you. The actions which distressed that old lady have no bearing whatsoever on your standing in Christ. They have not changed your salvation. You can't be "unborn-again"!'

'But I feel condemned,' I argued. 'I hurt her—and I often do wrong things.'

'So do I,' confessed my patient fiancé. 'But I don't allow the Devil to keep making me feel guilty. I confess my sin and get rid of it.'

Looking back, it is surprising that someone who had read the Scriptures for years should be so ignorant. I had been saved by grace, but I was still seeking to live not by faith but by good works. So when my good works failed, I was very vulnerable to condemnation. Gradually, I learned to believe that what the Bible said was true. I was *not* a slave to sin. I did not habitually, wilfully and deliberately live a life that was Godless or self-centred. My normal life was to live righteously and it became my desire to live from my new born-again spirit.

I had to understand that my new born-again spirit is encased in a body of flesh, and sometimes, instead of subduing it, I indulge it. Previously, that would have thrown me into schizophrenic confusion. 'I'm saved, I know I am.'

'But you sinned.'

'I didn't mean to. I'll try harder.'

'But you can't be a Christian if you sin.'

'Give me time. I promise I'll improve, and then I'll come back to God.'

'You'll do it again, you know you will. You're absolutely hopeless! You'll never be free!'

Condemnation is one of Satan's strongest and deadliest weapons and it is effective because believers do not know the truth about their standing in Christ. I have learned that I have a choice; I do not have to let sin rule my life. I do not have to listen to Satan's lies. He says, 'You're no good. You can't be a Christian.' I say, 'The Bible says I am new inside, I am born again, I am dead to sin, I am dead to law, but I am alive to Christ.' I can exercise my freedom.

But what if a Christian *does* sin? Doesn't that negate everything? No. It means that he has willingly given in to temptation. He was not powerless or compelled to do wrong—he just did not employ his freedom, either through ignorance, choice or weakness.

Terry explained this very helpfully. 'It's like living in a house called freedom from sin,' he said. 'This is our normal environment, a place where we have freedom, security, a sense of belonging and the right to be there. Now, if we sin, we are not thrown out and denied entrance ever again. At the back of the house is a fire escape, and over the top is written 1 John 2:1, "If anyone sins, we have an Advocate with the Father.... If we confess our sins, He is faithful and righteous to forgive us our sins and to cleanse us." We do not use this door all the time—it is there for the occasional emergency.'

The normal Christian life is biased not towards sin but towards righteousness. Our old nature has died and we are no longer enslaved to sin (Rom 6:6). However, because our new nature is still living in the flesh, which is vulnerable, we sometimes fall. We will never be totally free from 'the flesh' until 'this vile body' is exchanged for a glorious new one. That's why Paul says, 'We are eagerly waiting for our adoption, the redemption of our body.'

In the meantime, if and when we sin, we must not yield to the battering ram of condemnation from the Enemy. He cannot deprive us of our salvation but he can rob us of our joy. He can pile on the guilt and condemnation in such a heap that we feel very distant from our loving Father. It's all a trick, a big con! Jesus has made provision for us. Confess your sin, receive his forgiveness, and declare the truth—'There is no condemnation for those who are in Christ Jesus.'

Now—go and sin no more! 'You are no longer under law,' Jesus was effectively telling the woman caught in adultery. 'You are now under grace. Your guilt has been removed. When you came to me, you received not only forgiveness, but a new nature. Sin is foreign to this nature—you are no longer under its tyranny. I make you free.'

She did not know then that Jesus had covenanted with the Father to pay for her sin. Later, she would have heard about his arrest. Perhaps she was in the crowd that thronged the streets as he dragged his heavy cross over the stones. Perhaps she saw the dried blood from where the thorns were rammed into his head, caked onto his face, mixed with the sweat that poured down in the blistering heat. And perhaps she saw the wounds that the lash had made upon his back. He was paying the price that enabled her to go free.

At Jesus' trial, as he was dragged forward and made to stand before his accusers, there was no one to say, 'I do not condemn you.' Even his Father turned away. She should have died; she didn't. He need not have; he did. Her freedom, and yours, and mine, cost Jesus his life.

Perhaps that day, as he doodled in the dust while she stood guilty before him, he was weighing it up. The debt had to be paid. If she did not pay it, he would have to. Was she worth it?

He paid.

3

Freedom from Bondage

In her dream, she was walking tall and straight through a grassy meadow, her head held high, her limbs moving with effortless grace. Someone called her name and she began to run freely and easily through the spring flowers—then she tripped and fell. The dream faded and she floated up through layers of consciousness and re-entered the reality of pain and constriction that had been her life for eighteen years. Imprisoned in her bent and crippled body, the only freedom she knew was in her dreams.

It was the Sabbath. Today she would go to the synagogue. She lay twisted in her bed, summoning the strength for the ordeal of crawling out and getting dressed. She had stiffened up as she slept and now every movement was agony. Slowly, painfully, she inched her way to a sitting position and fumblingly dressed herself. Her shaking hand found the stick which was her constant support and, leaning upon it, she shuffled across the room to the corner where the bread bin lay. Nearly all her possessions had to be kept on the floor or on very low shelves because try as she would, she could not uncurl her spine to reach anything higher than her waist.

The little boy from next door knocked and entered. He was carrying a drink and some fruit which his mother, a busy but compassionate soul, had sent for her. He waited until 'the little lady', as he called her, had settled herself on a chair, then put the food on a low table beside her and squatted down, watching her with bright, curious eyes. Nobody else seemed to have much time for her, but he liked her because she was small. In fact, he was taller than she was—even when she was standing up! It made him feel big and important. But she was a funny shape!

She finished the drink and he jumped up to take the cup. But instead of skipping off as he usually did, he hovered, fidgeting. His mum would probably have scolded him for asking, but he had to know. Shyly, but with a child's directness, he asked, 'Why is your back bent like that?'

Bent as she was, her line of vision was confined mainly to the floor and she had to twist awkwardly to look at him. She sighed, and he was relieved that she did not look cross at his bold question. Not many people saw her face. He probably saw it more than most, and he hardly ever saw a smile on it. On this occasion, however, she did smile and he noted with interest that some of the big lines almost disappeared.

She did not mind telling him. Not many people had time to talk to her and still fewer could remember her when she had been as straight and normal as they were. But she must be careful not to talk too much or she would be late at the synagogue. It took her such a long time to get there!

'I was not always like this,' she told the curious child. 'I used to be able to run and skip like you. My back was straight and I could hold up my head and look around and see everything just like everyone else! I used to play games with my friends and as I grew older I used to help my mother in the house and look after the younger children. I was hoping to marry and have my own children one day.' The smile had gone now and she sighed wistfully. He did not know that she was back in her dream in the flower-filled meadow where the voice that called her name seemed to her to be sweet and tender and full of promise.

Her eyes were sad and dull as she continued. 'But I was often very tired and my legs sometimes hurt unbearably. I would get terrible pains in my bones, especially in my back. My mother would often chide me for not standing straight. "Stand up child!" she would say. "Pull your shoulders back. You're stooping again," and I would try. But it was as if a great weight had come upon my shoulders, forcing them down. I became weaker and weaker. My parents took me to many doctors, but no cure could be found. They said my bones were crumbling and fusing together and there was nothing they could do. One day, I fell and I could not get up. Friends carried me to my bed. That was eighteen years ago. I have been bent like this ever since.'

'Oh,' replied the little boy. He did not know what to say next, so he stood on one leg and poked his finger in his ear. Then a sudden idea floated into his head and straight out of his mouth. 'Maybe Jesus could help you—you know, straighten you out. My mum says he's coming today.' Blithely, he ran out into the sun, cup in hand.

She sat still for some moments, trying to gather strength for the next move. She was locked so rigidly that every movement brought fresh waves of pain and drained the energy from her. Telling the child about the tragic events of eighteen years ago had reminded her of the pain inside that she had sought to bury. She remembered how the darkness had closed in on her as she lay on that bed; the loneliness and sorrow as she grieved for the lost hopes; the bitterness that had risen up inside her like an animal that would not be tamed. The heaviness of spirit was almost as bad as the pain in her body.

Eighteen years! 'I've been robbed!' she told herself vehemently. 'Robbed of happiness, fulfilment, a husband, children. Robbed of the normal things that people take for granted! I can't move freely. I can't even see the world around me—only the ground!'

The boy had talked about Jesus. She had heard of him. Stories had been circulating around the towns and villages about blind people seeing, deaf hearing, lame walking—all healed by Jesus, a man from Nazareth. Well, maybe there was a chance that he could 'straighten her out' as the lad had put it. Whether he could heal her crooked back or the tangle in her soul, she did not know—either would be a miracle—but she would go to the synagogue anyway.

Resolutely, she pulled herself up again and, leaning on her stick, left her house and began the arduous journey to the synagogue. It was not far, but it exacted all the energy she had. She felt the sun, warm upon her back, but could not look up as she toiled along the dusty road. People hurried by, some calling a greeting to her. She knew them by their voices and their feet. She did not know their faces.

They had already begun to recite the Psalms as she tapped and creaked her way to a seat behind the screen in the women's quarters. She sank down onto the seat and shut her eyes. It took her some while to recover, but eventually she became aware of a new voice. The words were familiar, but they came with a force and a passion that imbued them with freshness and relevance. He spoke about the crooked being made straight and about captives being set free! Boldly, he declared that the Spirit of the Lord had anointed him to do these things.

There was an incredulous silence. The people knew the scriptures. They knew that these passages referred to the Messiah, the One who would come from God to be the Deliverer of his people. Never before had anyone dared to claim that these scriptures applied to himself! And yet, they had to admit that he spoke with authority. He did not suggest, imply or mention possibilities. He made clear, unequivocal statements.

'This day has this scripture been fulfilled in your ears!' The proclamation released a variety of reactions. Some were nodding, their eyes growing wide with wonder and excitement as the implications of this statement began to dawn upon them. Others muttered angrily, their faces heavy with frowns. The noise increased as shouts of approval mingled with roars of fury.

Suddenly, that clear voice cut through the hubbub, 'Woman!' A tremor went through her. For a moment she had thought he was calling her. But instantly she answered herself, 'Impossible! He doesn't know you, and why would he single you out—despised, small, disfigured as you are? And there are lots of other women in here.'

'Woman!' There was an insistency and irresistibility in that call. She knew, as if there were no one else in the room, that he was calling her. Deep inside, she knew. She had to respond, though it cost her greatly. She felt for her stick on the floor and laboriously levered herself up to start the agonising, embarrassing journey towards him. Slowly, she inched her way through the excited people who were continuing their heated exchanges on the merits of the sermon and the preacher. Slowly, slowly, she tapped and shuffled through the throng and gradually the clamour ceased as she reached the centre where he stood. There was silence.

All she could see of the preacher was his sandalled feet and the hem of his robe. His voice rang out clearly above her head. It was not a prayer, a plea or a hope, but a statement, a pronouncement: 'Woman, you are freed!'

In her heart, something was unlocked. He laid his hands on her poor, bent back. Power flowed down her spine like warm water. She knew she could move! She lifted her head and her shoulders. As she did so, the knotted-up muscles and fused joints loosened and relaxed. For the first time in eighteen years, she stood tall and erect. Now she was not looking at his feet. She was gazing into his face—a face that radiated joy and delight in what he had done.

She was healed! She was free! A stronger power than her sickness had invaded her. She lifted her hands in worship, tears spilling down her face and incoherent words of thankfulness pouring from her heart.

She was barely aware of the uproar that ensued.

Amid the shouts of amazement, the voice of the synagogue official cut through with glacial disapproval. 'There are six other days in the week to get healed. This is work that should not be done on the Sabbath!' There was a chorus of agreement from others standing around.

Looking at them, Jesus replied, 'You hypocrites! You would not leave your donkey tied up on the Sabbath, would you? You would untie him and lead him to water! Now, this woman is a daughter of Abraham. Satan has bound her for eighteen long years! Is it not right that she should be released on the Sabbath?'

The official and his cronies were disconcerted. The crowd was jubilant. Chattering and laughing, they surged out of the synagogue to spread the news of this new wonder.

The woman, feeling strangely tall, left her stick lying on the floor and began to walk to the door, delighting in the ease of movement and absence of pain. The little boy from next door was waiting for her. He looked up at her and grinned. 'You're taller than me now!' he said. 'But I don't mind,' he added handsomely.

The happy crowd closed around her and the day was filled with joy and laughter as neighbours and friends relived the morning's events and begged her to tell them again and again. 'What did it feel like when he touched you?' and, 'What does it feel like now?'

Patiently, she told them over and over, but she was secretly relieved when evening came and they drifted off to their homes. She was beginning to feel weary with all the excitement and she needed some solitude to think over what had happened. Privately, she wanted to relive it all: the moment she heard him call her, the slow but deliberate journey of response and then that authoritative declaration, 'You are freed!'

What had happened then? She knew something had left her, an invisible, malevolent presence that had been like a suffocating parasite all these years. Then when Jesus had laid his hands on her, she felt in her body the manifestation of that release.

She pondered his words, 'this daughter of Abraham'. That's what he had called her. She had never thought of herself like that. To be a woman was to be second-rate in Jewish thinking, but to be a bent, weak, deformed woman was to be rated as particularly insignificant. She was useless, good for nothing! But Jesus had not seen her like that. He had given her the dignity of a name, 'daughter of Abraham'. He saw her as a child of the covenant and therefore worthy of regard and entitled to the healing available in the covenant. She revelled in that rediscovered identity and rejoiced that now she would be able to walk with her head held high in regal dignity.

Then there was the revelation that even daughters of Abraham could be enslaved, that it was Satan who had bound her. He had been responsible for these years of agony and bondage. He had sent his minions and imprisoned her in her crippled body and had caused her to suffer the cruel abuse of other hideous demons: humiliation, rejection, self-contempt, frustration and bitterness. For eighteen years they had kept up their relentless torment. She had been robbed of the delights of normal movement, vision and family life. Indignation rose up in her. How dare he so enslave a daughter of Abraham!

Yet there were other people who were not physically crippled but who were fully aware and proud of their identity as sons of Abraham. Jesus told these people that they also were slaves. 'You shall know the truth and the truth shall make you free,' he had declared.

'We are Abraham's offspring,' his opponents had retorted indignantly. 'We have never been enslaved. Why do you say we shall become free?' Jesus explained that whoever commits sin is enslaved by it and that for a slave there is no liberty. Only the son of the household has the authority to liberate slaves and 'if the Son sets you free, you are truly free'. Then he told them, 'I know that technically you are Abraham's descendants, but my word is not finding any response in your hearts. Be like Abraham who received God's word and lived by it. If you cannot hear and receive my word, you belong to Satan. You are enslaved by him and he is a liar and a murderer.'

Many women today are in bondage to Satan. They are enslaved by sin, they are tangled in lies, they have been robbed of their freedom in many ways. Some know that they have desperate needs, but do not know how to escape. Others do not even know that they are bound and are consequently unaware that they need to be freed. Still others feel oppressed, but attribute their oppression to other causes: poverty, domination by men, environmental problems, inadequate education or political factors, such as laws governing property, wages and divorce.

Undoubtedly, there are many wrongs which need to be righted. It is, however, hopeless for us to try to change our society if we do not identify the root of all these problems. The root is slavery to sin and the slave master is Satan.

The presence of decay and corruption and disease in the human body also owes its origin to Satan, although not all sickness is the direct result of demonic activity. Satan has been active in distorting, destroying and enslaving God's creation ever since the Garden of Eden. Once the principle of rebellion towards God was set in motion, it affected every part of our tripartite beings. The contamination deadened the human spirit, making it impossible to respond to God, let alone enjoy fellowship with him or please him. The mind became set on the flesh, hostile towards God, and in our mortal bodies death began to reign.

The human race was under a curse until Jesus died on the cross, took the curse upon himself and broke its power. We can now learn to take authority over the Enemy and his demons. The Son has set us free. We have been adopted as sons and therefore have the right to use the Son's authority. We can walk in freedom ourselves and bring freedom to others.

Many people need the fundamental release of being born again. Many others who are already born again will be surprised and disconcerted to find that although they are sons and daughters of Abraham, so to speak, they can still be enslaved. Their spirits are not bound since these are entirely new. Rather, it is in the soulish areas—which are now being reclaimed and cleaned up—that nasty things are uncovered.

These had existed quite happily in the unregenerate person, but now that he is regenerate, they cannot stay dormant indefinitely. The life of the Holy Spirit inevitably exposes unholy things and they have to be dealt with. These 'unholy things' can be habits, patterns of thinking, submerged emotional pain, fears and wrong perceptions of God.

God's word has given clear guidance on how to grow up in him. He has given us weapons so that we can conduct successful warfare. He tells us that our enemies are the world, the flesh and the Devil.

We overcome the world by 'setting our minds on things above, where Christ is'. In other words, we employ prayer, discipline and the application of God's word to retrain our thought patterns and appetites.

We overcome the flesh by walking in the Spirit, by resisting temptation and by obeying Jesus.

We overcome the Devil and his demons by submitting to God and telling the Enemy to flee. Sometimes he has a firm foothold in a Christian's life. He has tormented that person for a long time and will not willingly surrender the ground that he has claimed. This is where the gift of discernment of spirits comes into effect. The Enemy is a master of disguise and we can easily be fooled into thinking that the root cause of our problem is anything but demonic. But when he is 'sussed out' by the Holy Spirit, he has to go.

Jesus has purchased our freedom, but so often we continue in bondage. This happens either because we are unaware that we are being harassed by demons, or because we are unwilling to accept the possibility that Christians can be subjected to demonic activity.

Naturally, we must not blame all our failures and shortcomings on the presence of demons. We are accountable to God for sin, which must be confessed, repented of and cleansed away. However, where there is a problem area which does not yield to the normal disciplines, we can suspect the work of a demon. This is not something to cause us shame; rather, we should be grateful that a diagnosis has been made! Now freedom is in sight! We have the authority of Jesus to get rid of the unwanted squatter!

In 1985, I was attending a conference in San Diego, California, where John Wimber was the speaker. I had been troubled by anger which used to flare up within me, frightening me and others by its savage intensity. I remember hurling things around my bedroom as a teenager and weeping with rage and frustration. Once, I got hold of one of my sisters and shook her so violently, that I frightened myself as much as her. Inside me was a rage, spurring me on to such an extent that I knew I had the capacity for...what? Only God knows what his grace restrained me from doing.

After I was baptised in the Spirit I knew I could keep the urge down and under control, but it was unpredictable and suddenly I would find myself in the grip of searing, intense frustration. I began to recognise other feelings linked with it: intolerance of various forms of weakness in people, and an urge always to be in the front, at the centre, to the extent that I would do stupid things to be noticed. Somehow, it was preferable to be seen, even as a clown, than not to be seen at all.

I had wept and sought God many times about these hateful traits, but could not seem to grow out of them, ignore them or become free of them.

Then one evening at this conference, there was a prophecy about the wind of the Spirit blowing across the auditorium. A word of knowledge came that the Lord wanted to heal women suffering from pre-menstrual tension. This had never been much of a problem to me, so I watched with interest as droves of women went to the front. I was astounded when it seemed as if wind blew upon them from one side of the room to the other. Some laughed, some cried and some dropped to the floor. Everyone was touched.

Then John Wimber told husbands present to turn and pray for their wives. Terry turned to me and began to pray. Neither of us was sure what to pray for and after a few minutes, he stopped and said, 'Shall I go on or shall we leave now?' I said perhaps he should go on praying because I had a funny feeling that there was more to come. For some reason, Terry placed his hands on my stomach and said, 'Oh God, break whatever needs to be broken.'

Suddenly, I was engulfed by such a tremendous wave of pent-up frustration that I began to gasp and cry out. It seemed to me that I was a tiny little girl crouched up at one end of a tunnel. The words came to me so clearly, 'It's all right. You are only a little girl. You can cry if you want to.'

I became aware of someone calling my name and struggled up through layers of consciousness to see several concerned faces staring at me. 'What's going on?' someone asked. I described what I had seen. Then it dawned on me that it all had something to do with my being the first-born of four children—having to strive to perform; to stay out front; to be the leader and not let anyone overtake me. 'Yes!' said one of the counsellors. 'I think you need to be released from the torments of a competitive spirit.' Then he commanded my release in the name of Jesus.

I felt unsteady and light-headed, but I was unprepared for what happened next. I felt a wave of terrible remorse for the injury I must have inflicted on many people by my behaviour. I wept tears of repentance and as I received Jesus' forgiveness, I knew I was clean and free.

The next day I felt strange—raw, vulnerable and uncertain about what had taken place. Was it all an illusion? Had I undergone some sort of emotional manipulation? I was greatly heartened when I read in 1 Thessalonians 5, 'In everything give thanks; for this is God's will for you in Christ Jesus. Do not quench the Spirit; do not despise prophetic utterances. But examine everything carefully; hold fast to that which is good.'

If it was of God, it would stand up to scrutiny and would bear fruit. In the weeks that followed, I felt a buoyancy and joy as if I had just been saved. I fell in love with Jesus all over again and could truly say that it no longer mattered to me who had the limelight.

That blinding, choking rage has gone. My family know that there are times when I am irritable and short-tempered—I need to concentrate on the fruits which are gentleness and patience, but that driving force which suddenly used to rear its head has gone.

I do not believe I was demon-possessed, but as I understand it, ever since I was a little child I had been harassed and tormented by agents of the Enemy. They could not possess me because I belonged to Jesus, but for a long time they rode on my back. Then, when exposed and confronted by the authority of Jesus, they had to go.

I am a liberated lady!

4

Freedom from Unbelief

Sarah leaned against the door post of the tent and stared hopelessly at the desert landscape. Twilight was falling and it all looked grey and dreary and featureless which just about summed up the way she felt about herself.

'I used to be beautiful,' she thought, and sighed as she remembered the devious methods Abraham had employed on two occasions to conceal the fact that she was his wife, lest jealousy and lust should provoke murder—his murder! Yes, she had been a notable beauty and when she had become Abraham's wife back in the Chaldean city of Ur, she had expected a life very different from this!

However, she had submitted willingly to Abraham's strange desire for the nomadic life, understanding that he was leaving one city in order to seek another: one that God was building, he said! She was not totally clear what this meant, but what she had grasped eagerly was that he had received a promise from God. This promise was that he would be the father of a nation which would be as innumerable as the sand upon the seashore. This was where she came in—if there was to be a father, there had to be a mother too!

'I was not only beautiful,' she thought sadly, 'I was full of hope as well. I was going to be a mother. In fact not just any mother, but a very important mother—the mother of a nation—only it never happened.'

Half dreaming as she stood in the twilight by the tent door, she remembered the high hopes with which they had set out for their new life. They didn't know where they were going, but God had called, so they had obeyed. But it was not long before the rigours of desert life hit them and the romance began to wear thin. For one thing, they were always looking for pasture and water. Everywhere they went they were accompanied by ever-increasing herds of sheep and cattle which in no time devoured every blade of grass in sight. So they were constantly on the move. It got very tiring. Sarah began to wish they had a more settled existence. She got fed up with the demands of sheep, the noise of sheep and the smell of sheep. Even their diet was always the same—bread and sheep!

Then there were the quarrels between Abraham's herdsmen and the herdsmen of Lot who was Abraham's nephew. Lot also had considerable flocks and herds and it became increasingly difficult for the land to support both companies if they continued to travel together. Finally, they had parted.

After Lot had left, life was more peaceful, but it was not uneventful. Abraham and Sarah were involved in several escapades: Lot had to be rescued when he was captured by a coalition of five kings. Then there was an encounter with Melchizedek, King of Salem. Sadly, the event they most longed for seemed as though it would never happen—the birth of a son.

Sarah sat down heavily on a stool and recalled her dejection after ten years of wandering in Canaan with no sign of a child. Abraham had reminded her of God's repeated promises but in vain. Her hope had shrivelled and died. She no longer had faith in those promises.

About that time, Hagar had come into her service. She was young and her dark skin was smooth and wrinkle-free. Her hair was long and glossy with none of the grey hairs that Sarah now had. Her eyes were dark and inviting. Somehow it was obvious that she was fertile.

Sarah considered the situation. Her body had aged, ravaged by the dust and desert winds. She felt old, she looked old and she knew that she was old—too old now to become pregnant. Her menstrual cycle, always erratic and uncertain, had ceased entirely but Abraham wanted, needed, a son. There had to be another way! Hagar had to be the answer.

But it was the biggest mistake she and Abraham had ever made. Even now Sarah winced as she remembered the sly, triumphant sneer on the face of the now pregnant Hagar. She had conceived so easily! 'Look at me,' she seemed to say as she stroked her swollen abdomen. 'I'm normal. I'm fertile. I can do what you can't do. I'm *someone* now.'

Jealousy, anger and self-pity had inflamed Sarah. They had quarrelled violently and she had sent the girl packing. Hagar had fled into the wilderness, had nearly died of thirst but had reappeared much chastened after her ordeal. Eventually, the child was born and was named Ishmael.

That was thirteen years ago. Slowly, Sarah pulled herself up to her feet. She looked out at the now darkened landscape and up at the stars, then she turned to go in. It had been a long and momentous day. Abraham and his son Ishmael had been circumcised. They had received in their bodies the mark of God's covenant.

What covenant? Abraham had told her that a few days ago God had repeated to him that he would bless him and his descendants. 'Oh that Ishmael might live before you,' Abraham had cried. 'I will bless him,' replied God, 'but he is not to be your heir. Sarah will have a son.'

It was all too much. Shaking her head, Sarah wished the cruel joke would die. She was old, tired, useless and she ached from head to foot. She went to bed.

A few days later, it was Abraham who was sitting at the tent door, dozing in the noon heat. The horizon now was a shimmering haze and all was quiet and still.

Something roused him out of his reverie. He looked up and was startled to find three men standing nearby. 'I didn't hear them coming,' he thought, surprised. 'I must have dropped right off. Wherever did they come from?' Collecting his scattered wits, he stumbled to his feet and hurried to greet them. The desert was an inhospitable place. All who lived and travelled in it knew its harsh and savage nature and a code existed among them to give shelter and refreshment to any who passed near their tent.

Abraham invited the strangers to pause on their travels and take time to rest and eat. He was currently encamped at an oasis called Mamre where a grove of oak trees gave sweet relief from the merciless sun. He settled his guests under a tree and went to instruct Sarah and the servants to prepare a meal.

As he went to his herd to select a choice calf, he was still pondering the strangely sudden arrival of these three men. In the desert one usually knew about the approach of a traveller for some time before he actually arrived. Even a small cloud of dust could be visible for miles. But these three were unheralded by hoofbeats or dustclouds. They appeared not to have camels or horses. They were simply, suddenly there!

In due course, the calf was butchered, dressed and roasted, and the bread was kneaded and cooked. The food was carried to the guests where they sat in the shade of the oak tree. There was little talking while the meal was eaten. Then one of them looked up at his host with a smile and wiped his fingers. 'Where is Sarah, your wife?' he asked courteously.

'She's in the tent,' replied Abraham, thinking that his guests wanted to compliment her on the succulence of the meat, the flavour of the cheese and the warm, crusty bread. Sarah was an expert by now. She knew one hundred and one ways of presenting lamb and calf! He made as if to go and fetch her, but was checked as the man began to speak again. Afterwards, for the life of him, he couldn't remember which one it was. There was something about them that was different... or similar. They all seemed the same, yet they were distinctly three separate people. But surely he had heard that voice before?

No matter which one it was speaking, they were obviously all in agreement. 'I will surely return to you at this time next year and, behold, Sarah shall have a son.'

It certainly wasn't the first time he had heard this

promise, but never before had a time been attached to it. He heard a splutter behind him and knew that Sarah, hidden behind the door, had also heard.

Sarah had indeed heard. From where she was standing in the shadows of the tent, she could see her husband bent, grey and bearded. Suddenly, the thought of this elderly figure becoming a father seemed comical. The hand that flew to her mouth to suppress the bubble of laughter which was rising in her was wrinkled and heavily veined. 'I'm as bad,' she thought hysterically, looking at it. 'We're a couple of old dears. Why, I'm past conceiving and Abraham's probably past seeing any action too. It would be a laugh even trying!'

While she was trying to stifle the laughter that was threatening her composure, Abraham was struck dumb as he grappled with the implication of what these strangers were saying. How did they know about Sarah? How could they be so sure she would have a baby? Only God could know that.... Who were they?

The next words rang out clearly, so that Sarah, shaking with laughter in the tent with her hands over her face, heard them. 'Why did Sarah laugh saying, "Shall I, indeed, have a child when I am so old?"? Is anything too difficult for the Lord?'

Suddenly, she no longer felt like laughing. As quickly as it had arisen, her mirth ceased and a kind of fear settled on her instead. Impulsively, she stepped out into the sun and said nervously, 'I didn't laugh.' Gently, the voice insisted, 'No, but you did laugh.' Trembling, she retreated into the tent. Later, when she looked out, the men had gone.

Nothing much seemed to happen for the next three months, but Sarah could not dismiss the incident from her mind, and neither could Abraham. At first, they looked at each other helplessly: two old people who loved each other deeply but for whom physical union was a thing of the past.

Abraham was nearly one hundred years old now. He thought about his body and about what was necessary in order to father a child. He had to admit it—in that respect he was as good as dead (Rom 4:19–20). There was absolutely no chance of his fathering a son, let alone Sarah mothering one! He faced the facts, but then he faced the promise of God. He knew he had a choice to make. He could either believe what the physical facts told him: that to have a child was impossible, or he could believe God's promise. The Scriptures say, 'He did not waver in unbelief, but grew strong in faith, giving glory to God' (v 20).

It was more than thirteen years since Ishmael had been conceived. But God had spoken, so Abraham put his trust in him. The more he meditated on God's promise and God's character, the stronger his faith grew, fuelled by his worship.

It took longer for Sarah. She needed to be freed from total unbelief. Hope had long since died within her and in its place had come a flatness, a sense of disillusionment and resignation. She had learned to live with the status quo. The fact that she had not had any children was one of life's mysteries. The sharpness of the pain had subsided long ago and she had grown so used to the dull ache of disappointment that she hardly noticed it any more.

But now this visit had stirred it all up again. She felt unsettled. She didn't want to think about it, but she couldn't get it out of her mind. 'It's absurd,' she kept telling herself firmly. 'It's too late now. Look at you, that part of your life is over. You are well past the age of child-bearing. It's impossible!'

One morning, she was kneading the dough. She pounded it savagely as, once again, she tried to press the issue out of her mind. 'Impossible! Impossible!' She banged out the rhythm as she kneaded. She put the dough in a warm place to rise, sat down for a rest and closed her eyes. Into her mental orbit swam the vision of those three strangers and she heard again, 'Nothing is impossible with God.'

Gradually, over the next few weeks, her focus changed. She found that she was thinking less about herself and her inadequacies and more about God and his unlimited ability. She had to work through some of the blockages that were obstructing faith. One was her sense of failure. She had grown so used to being a failure that she found it hard to see herself as an achiever. But she found that as she contemplated those words, 'nothing is impossible with God', her failures were swallowed up. It was God who would do it. He wasn't a failure, he was always a success! The fact that up to now she had been unable to conceive was irrelevant. With God, it was now possible.

But there was also her jealousy and anger towards Hagar. Sarah now felt that she had reacted badly in that relationship, so why should God do anything for her? Her guilt was like a mountain blocking her understanding—until again God's word came to her rescue. He had not said anything about her worthiness. He had simply stated that she would have a son. He had chosen her despite all her weaknesses, because it suited his purposes. In fact, her imperfections only made his grace more wonderful.

One night, she lay gazing at the stars, awesome in their twinkling millions, and was reminded of God's promise to her husband: that his descendants would be as innumerable as those stars. Once they had not existed. Then he spoke and they did. It came to her then that if by a word God could cause those stars to spring into existence, was it so unthinkable that out of a dead womb he could bring forth life—life that would spawn countless generations? The thought took her breath away.

Abraham had believed the God who called things that were not as though they were (Rom 4). Now it was her turn. It was amazing that God could speak and thereby bring something into existence. But even more breathtaking was the thought that the only thing preventing it happening was her lack of co-operation. She had to take a leap of faith. She had to believe God for the impossible.

God was big—bigger than her failure, her barren womb, her jealousy and weakness. He was the creator of the stars and the world. He was the giver of life! She exulted in his greatness. How absurd it was to think that anything was impossible when he had given his word! Hope surged up through her spirit and she laughed for joy. This was not the cynical laughter of the sceptic, but the joy of one liberated from unbelief to faith by the revelation of God's word.

She went into the tent. Abraham was waiting for her. He looked at his beloved wife and knew that something profound had happened to her. He led her to the bed.

News came of the destruction of the city of Sodom. How had Lot fared? Abraham and Sarah waited anxiously. Eventually a messenger arrived, breathless, with an account of Lot's last minute escape with his daughters. Sadly, his wife had lingered and had been overtaken by the disaster.

Sarah suddenly felt faint and nauseous. She sat down, trembling. Was it just the news that made her feel that way? The next day she was sick when she awoke. She was pregnant.

Isaac was born a year after the visit of the three strangers. The ninety-year-old mother looked up at the one-hundred-year-old father and smiled. 'God has made laughter for me,' said she. 'Everyone who hears will laugh with me' (Gen 21:6).

5

Freedom from Frustration

Angry tears slid down her cheeks and plopped into the gravy she was stirring with a wooden spoon. Hastily, she wiped them away with the back of her hand and forced down the sob that was threatening to engulf her. With iron control, she denied herself the indulgence of releasing her frustration. There was no time for that now! But her determination wavered perilously as she caught sight of the pile of greasy cooking pots, the unswept floor and the unlaid table. So much to do!

She wiped her hands on her apron and scurried over to the cupboard to fetch some clean plates. On the way, she had to pass the open door and through it she heard the low murmur of voices and glimpsed her sister Mary seated on a low stool, chin cupped in her hands, listening intently to the conversation.

Blinking hard, Martha rushed over to baste the joint

of roasting lamb. Mentally, she listed the other things that had to be done before the meal was ready to be served: check seating arrangements; put the bread on platters; finish the dessert; wash the fruits—the drinks! She had nearly forgotten the drinks. Oh, why did all the vegetables have to come to the boil at the same moment?

Frantically, she grabbed a cloth and tried to mop up the overflow from a steaming cooking pot. Somehow, in her hurry and tension, she upset a plateful of carefully chopped herbs which were intended to garnish the lamb. They fluttered down and mixed with the other debris on the unswept floor. Her vision of a perfectly cooked and beautifully presented meal vanished. It was the last straw.

All day she had been busily cooking, chopping, mixing and stirring. She had so wanted to set a worthy meal before Jesus and his disciples. She had been fuelled by a rosy picture in which she served her guests with a dinner surpassing in succulence and flavour anything that they had eaten before, in an atmosphere of total calm and composure. She would receive their compliments with dignity and retire humbly to the kitchen, in the knowledge that her reputation as a gracious hostess and fabulous cook would travel far and wide.

'It's all for him,' she told herself. 'And now this!' The kitchen was in chaos, the vegetables overdone, the lamb half raw, the table still unlaid and now the finishing touches scattered on the floor. It was too much. No one could expect her to do all the work. Why couldn't someone see that she needed some help? Of course, she couldn't, she wouldn't, ask for it. But they should have realised!

Mary's tuneful laugh rang out and all Martha's frustration surfaced. It was all Mary's fault. Why couldn't she lend a hand instead of idling the day away and putting herself forward in front of the guests like that?

Martha marched to the door and stood, hands on hips. 'Master!' she exploded. 'Don't you care that I am doing all the work? Why don't you tell Mary to come and help me?'

Startled, the guests turned towards her and then back to Jesus who was seated at the far end of the room. Everyone waited for him to send Mary back to the kitchen where she belonged.

Jesus looked at Martha's hot, flushed face and saw the frustration and resentment in her heart. He saw beneath the tension to the ache of unfulfilment; the longing to be recognised and appreciated; the attempt to buy his approbation with an excess of serving. He saw that her elaborate preparations, although ostensibly for him, were really an effort to win affirmation, to find an identity in doing something well, and now it had all backfired—poor Martha!

He wanted her to make a discovery. 'If I am really at the centre, you don't need to strive for fulfilment. You will find it in me if you put me first.' But he didn't say that. He put out his hand and smiled at her. As he drew her towards himself, he spoke quietly so that only the nearest could hear his words. 'Martha, Martha, you are so anxious about lots of things, but really only a few are necessary. In fact, only one thing is important. Mary has found it and I am not going to deny it to her. She has made the right choice.'

This radical gear change was not what Martha wanted to hear. It was an entirely new perspective that he was offering. Her panic had not pressurised him into instant action. He didn't send a humiliated, guilt-ridden Mary away from his feet. He did not offer an answer for the immediate crisis. He was forcing her to review her entire lifestyle!

He held her eyes for a few minutes. She managed a wobbly smile of response and murmured something about dinner being slightly delayed. It didn't seem to matter very much any more, not when he looked at her like that—so kind and understanding.

He turned his gaze away from her and continued his teaching while she retreated thoughtfully to the kitchen. The tension had gone out of her, but she did not feel deflated. While she sorted out the muddle and finished preparing the meal, her mind was grappling with a new concept. Things that had so consumed her up until now suddenly seemed...trivial? Insignificant? No, just secondary instead of primary.

'One thing.' What was the 'one thing' that he had called necessary? It must be something precious indeed—particularly if it were to replace the many things that filled her life and caused her to be anxious. He said that Mary had chosen it. Martha was puzzled. What had Mary chosen that was so special? What was Mary doing that she, Martha, was not doing? Only sitting at Jesus' feet listening to him.

Was that what he meant? Was that the golden key? 'But,' thought Martha indignantly, 'if we all sat around all day, nothing would get done. Someone's got to do the work!' She picked up the water pitcher and started to cross the room, but stopped in her tracks as another thought struck her. He said 'one thing' is necessary. Perhaps if I stopped to listen to him, I would find out what that thing is. She continued her walk to the table and put down the pitcher. Again, she paused, straightened and surveyed the room full of all her work.

Did he mean, then, that this was all unnecessary? The thought hurt. Doesn't he want my service, then? Is he rejecting my efforts to please him?

Again, the voice persisted. 'How do you know what pleases him? You haven't got close enough to find out. You have simply assumed that what pleases you pleases him.'

It takes courage to be honest. Martha drew a deep breath and squared her shoulders. 'I didn't ask him,' she admitted to herself. 'Perhaps if I had asked him what he would have liked, he would have wanted something quite different. Maybe that is what I was afraid of—that he would be content with a simple meal prepared beforehand, whereas this ambitious feast was really to bolster my ego.'

Martha had complained about Mary, expecting Jesus to rebuke her for being idle and selfish. It was startling, therefore, to find that he commended Mary and turned the searchlight onto her sister! He did not demolish Martha by saying that all her labours were wrong. He did not tell her to abandon all her domestic chores. He did not say that Mary was spiritual and she was not. He did not downgrade her activities. He simply stated that she was bothered by many things, too many, and only a few were necessary. In other words, she could have cut down the detail and saved a lot of time and energy. In fact, if she got the 'one thing' right, everything else would find its level. 'Martha, rearrange your priorities! Mary has hers in the right order.'

What is the 'one thing' that Mary prized so highly, the 'one thing' Jesus commended her for, the 'one thing' he isolated as necessary? King David knew: 'One thing I have asked of the Lord and that shall I seek. That I may dwell in the house of the Lord all the days of my life. To behold the beauty of the Lord and meditate in his temple' (Ps 27:4).

When did he declare this? Was it at some point when, established as king, all problems were past and he had nothing to do all day but sit around in the temple? No! The previous verses speak of evil-doers devouring his flesh; of hosts encamping against him; of war arising all around him. 'In spite of this, I will be confident,' he asserts. 'And now my head will be lifted up above my enemies round about me. I will offer sacrifices with shouts of joy' (verse 6). Bravado? The power of positive thinking? The boasting of a super-ego? No again! He had a secret: a life of fellowship with God. Maintaining that fellowship was the 'one thing' that he prized above all else.

Fellowship is not a static thing confined only to quiet times. It is what the Bible refers to as 'walking' with him. It is not a legalistic observance, not a dutiful prayer, not a religious ritual. It is counting on his presence continually, cultivating it, enjoying it. God created Adam and Eve to walk and talk with him—that's fellowship.

I remember a time in my own life when I was stretched to the point of exhaustion. We were living in a large, three-storeyed house which required a lot of energy to keep in order. We had four young children, one of whom was an eighteen-month-old toddler. The other children were too young to go to school on their own, so every morning I had to rush to get them all fed, dressed and walked to school. I then pushed the baby home. In the afternoon, I had to go to the school again and walk back. We had numerous visitors and I was running a weekly women's meeting. My mother-in-law was in hospital too, so nearly every day I was taking my father-in-law to the other side of town to visit her. All the shopping, cooking and washing had to be fitted in somehow and I was getting very tired and frustrated.

A verse of Scripture kept running through my mind: 'My yoke is easy and my burden is light.' It was puzzling. What did it mean? My burden seemed anything but light. 'Come unto me all you who labour and are heavy laden and I will give you rest.' 'But Lord,' I kept protesting, 'that is exactly what I can't do. There isn't time to "come unto you". I know I should be praying and reading the word, but there isn't time! Some days I don't even sit down from breakfast time through to supper!'

Bit by bit, he reminded me of the rest of the verse. 'Take my yoke upon you and learn of me. I am gentle and humble, you will find rest for your soul.'

I had had a preconceived idea of fellowship with him. I thought it meant keeping up a good quiet time and if you didn't, you felt guilty. I had failed to realise that a yoke is made for a team, a partnership. I was struggling with my yoke alone. He was waiting for me to stop and draw near to him so that he could get under it and share the load. 'Don't shut me out,' he seemed to say. 'Let me in. Now is the time to draw near—while your hands are in the nappy bucket or while you are ploughing through the basket of ironing. Do it with me. You will find my yoke is easy and my burden is light.'

And I did, and I do. He is the King, but he is gentle and humble; humble enough to come to me and turn my most mundane tasks into moments of glory. I have had moments of ecstasy in meetings, but I have also had meetings of ecstasy in my kitchen.

Jesus chose the disciples to be with him, then he sent them out. First, he wanted their love and friendship. Their service was to spring out of that intimacy. John understood. He remembered Jesus' words in the Upper Room: 'If anyone loves Me, he will keep My word' (Jn 14:23). So if we are not enjoying his love, we will not be close enough to hear his word. We will do what we think his word is. We will reduce his word to formulae. We will live by rules instead of by a relationship. Jesus prayed like this: 'Father, I desire that they also, whom Thou hast given Me, be with Me where I am, in order that they may behold My glory' (Jn 17:24). Sadly, it is possible to belong to him without being with him. It is possible to be with him and yet not behold his glory. He is looking for a love relationship from which will spring our obedience and then he promises this: 'And My Father will love him, and We will come to him and make Our abode with him' (Jn 14:23).

It is wonderful when he comes to you where you are. What, come to the kitchen? Yes! To the dining room; the garden shed; the office? Yes! 'We will come.' Your kitchen, as you work at your despised sink and ironing board, can be full of the Trinity. The Father, Son and Holy Spirit will ride with you as you go to the shops. Your car can be the dwelling place of God. When you are next frustrated with your round of domesticity, invite his presence.

Martha soon experienced another sort of frustration. This time it was not caused by overwork while others apparently idled. If that had been a crisis, it was now cast into the shade by a catastrophe. Her brother Lazarus died.

Now Martha was not merely mopping up the gravy, she was faced with the shock and pain of bereavement. Most frustrating and perplexing of all was the thought, 'If only Jesus had got here quicker, Lazarus might have lived.' By the time Jesus turned up, Lazarus had been dead for four days. Why, oh why had he delayed? Why didn't he come when he was needed?

Martha was about to find out that our needs and panics cannot dictate to Jesus what he should do. He is not a press-button Saviour, an instant superman who rushes to the rescue when we blow the whistle.

'Don't you love us, Lord? Do you like seeing us hurt and bewildered?' That's the way we react when the Enemy taunts us. But Jesus always has an end in view that is much greater than anything we can envisage.

He knew that Martha's thinking was changing, but she hadn't yet received a full revelation of who he was. When she heard that he was coming, she couldn't sit still any longer. She had to see him. She had questions to ask. She was hurting. She felt bewildered.

'Lord, if you had been here, my brother would not have died!' An outburst of frustration and a statement of faith rolled into one. 'Lord, you could have healed him. Why didn't you?'

How many times have we blurted out something like that to God? We know he can heal; we know he can change a situation or make miraculous provision. We have even testified to our belief, and then he has left us apparently dangling in mid-air. He hasn't turned up. It's unfair. Why hasn't he honoured our commitment by doing what we expected?

Martha knew Jesus was a teacher. She knew he was a healer. Her next words revealed that she somehow knew there was more to him than that. Groping to understand, she exclaimed, 'Even now I know God will give you whatever you ask.' Simply, he stated, 'Your brother shall rise again.' She brushed it aside. 'Yes, I know he will rise in the Day of Resurrection.'

Then Jesus did what we would not dare to do. When someone is in the throws of grief, agonising in their bereavement, we put our arms around them, we comfort, we weep with them—and rightly. We do not seek to confront them with a huge new concept when they are in emotional turmoil.

Jesus dared. Jesus knew that now was the moment to stretch her perception of himself. The answer to her frustration lay in a fresh revelation of who he was. Once again, he switched her focus away from the problem. Before, he had made her re-examine her values. Now he made her look at him in a whole new light. 'I am the resurrection and the life. He who believes in me shall live, even if he dies, and everyone who believes in me shall never die. Do you believe this?'

The uncertainty, confusion, frustration, her preoccupation with her doubts and questions were all blown away by this breathtaking declaration. Before her stood the living, vital, wonderful Son of God. The revelation compelled an immediate response. 'Yes, Lord, I believe. You are the Christ, the Son of God, the One we have been waiting for.'

The word was near her. It was in her heart, in her mouth. As she confessed Jesus as Lord with her mouth and believed in her heart, something happened to her. She herself passed from death to life. It was enough. She went and called Mary. There was more than one resurrection that day. Later, many more believed as they actually saw Lazarus—once a dead man—walk out of the tomb at Jesus' command.

Six days before the Passover, Jesus returned to Bethany. Again, Martha served the supper, but she was a changed person. This was a family celebration. Lazarus was now reclining at the table, alive, healthy and no doubt with a hearty appetite. It was a joy to set a meal before him and Jesus, the two men she loved most. Now her serving sprang out of a heart full of love and gratitude. The atmosphere was so full of joy and thanksgiving that it seemed right and natural for Mary to fetch her most precious possession, a box of spikenard ointment, which she poured over the feet of Jesus. He received her worship and told those in the room with him that her gesture would be recorded for ever—just as Martha's service is recorded for us too.

The way we serve in our homes, families and churches can make it easier or harder for others to offer their worship.

Martha may have been more practical than Mary, but she was no less spiritual. Worship can express itself in many ways, but it springs from a heart that has encountered the One who is the Resurrection and the Life and which constantly walks with him.

Thomas à Kempis put it like this: 'When Jesus is present, all is well and nothing seems difficult, but when Jesus is absent, everything is arduous.'

6

Freedom from Bitterness

There was no denying it. She had become a crabby old woman. They had all remarked upon it as they gathered at the well before nightfall. 'I had been looking forward to seeing her again,' said one woman sadly. 'When we got word that she had decided to come back to Bethlehem again, I was quite excited.'

'Yes,' added another, 'so was I. It must be about ten years since she left.'

'At least that,' exclaimed a third. 'I was expecting my first baby then and she's almost into her teens now.'

They all fell into reminiscing as the buckets clanked up and down on the long rope. As the conversation drifted back to the original subject, they all felt the same shock about one thing: the change in Naomi.

Some of the younger ones barely remembered her. They had only been little girls during that terrible time of famine. What did stand out all too sharply was the memory of grinding hunger; the crying of little brothers and sisters who daily weakened, watched over by desperate mothers, themselves gaunt and weak. They could recall those pathetic cries subsiding as the babies became listless, lacking the energy to cry any more. Inevitably, many a morning would break to the heartrending discovery that a beloved infant had given up the struggle and that another lifeless little bundle would need to be buried by nightfall.

How they had lived through it was a marvel—something they did not care to think about too often. What determines the survival of one and the decline of another? The question would sometimes haunt them and they would grimly shrug it off and attend to the task of perpetuating the next link in the chain of humanity.

Yet the scarring of those famine years remained. The grotesque spectre of endless hunger haunted them. Now, they were overly watchful that their own children ate everything put in front of them and always kept something in reserve in their store cupboards. If the harvest was not too plentiful, they felt threatened again and all too carefully measured out the grain and the oil, praying that it would last. Oh yes, physically they had apparently recovered, but emotionally they were blighted by those childhood memories of famine.

In the height of that famine, one family had decided to escape while they had some strength left. It was a hard choice. Either they could stay and quite possibly starve to death, or they could take the drastic step of uprooting themselves, leaving all that was familiar and seeking another dwelling place where food was more plentiful.

Elimelech, Naomi's husband, was a bold and decisive man. He concluded that the cost of staying could be greater than going. So he took Naomi and his two sons, Mahlon and Chilion, to Moab. It had been a wrench leaving Bethlehem, not knowing if they would ever return. It had been hard carving out for themselves a new home among people who regarded them as strangers. Perhaps Naomi felt that, although physically they had come through the famine ordeal intact, she had nevertheless left behind something of herself in Bethlehem. Their little family unit became even more important as they applied themselves to building a new life together.

It was a devastating blow when after a few years Elimelech fell sick and died. Naomi was abruptly widowed. The lonely woman, already bereft of friends and family and now without a husband, became fiercely protective of her boys. They were her one link with the past. She clung to them and lived for them. Eventually, they married. She got on well with her two Moabite daughters-in-law and they loved and respected her. Although an air of sadness hovered about her, she must have been sufficiently like her name, 'pleasant', to cause them to feel comfortable with her. At last, life was beginning to have some constructive meaning for her. Then, suddenly, one after the other her precious sons also died.

The shock overwhelmed her. Orpah and Ruth, her daughters-in-law, now widowed themselves, wept with her. She was so distraught that they feared that her mind might become unstable. Bitterness and anger filled her soul. She turned away from all solace and retreated to her own shadowy cave of grief and pain. It seemed to her that her life had been one long tunnel of deepening agony. She gave up hope and abandoned herself to despair.

Word came that back in Judah the land was flourishing again. 'What have I got to lose?' thought Naomi sadly. 'I'll go back to Bethlehem.' Ruth and Orpah agreed that this was a good plan. 'It might take her out of herself,' suggested Orpah. 'Yes, returning to her old home might bring some comfort to her, poor thing,' said Ruth. 'But of course, she is in no condition to go alone. We must take her.'

Lovingly, they set about helping Naomi make preparations to leave. She was so absorbed in her grief that she almost forgot that they too had packing to do and farewells to say. Listlessly, she let them chivvy her into sorting out her possessions. The two young women cried again as they came across forgotten mementoes of their dead husbands. Naomi, however, would not cry any more. Her terrible grief had distilled into a hard lump of bitterness. What had she done to cause the Almighty to deal with her so harshly? She could not answer that question. Orpah and Ruth did not attempt to work it out either. They just loved her. She had been so good to them and they hated to see her in the grip of such depression. Perhaps returning to Bethlehem would help her.

So they all set out. Soon they reached the border between Moab and Judah. It did not seem to have sunk into Naomi's mind that her lovely daughters-in-law intended to go all the way home with her because she turned to them and began to say goodbye. 'You must go back to your own people now. May God bless you for all your kindness to me and my sons.'

'No, we're coming with you!' they protested.

Naomi persisted, 'You must go back and marry again.'

But they continued to protest and would not leave her. Her bitterness had made her cynical. 'Why should you come with me? What's in it for you? I'm too old to have a husband. Even if I had a husband tonight and conceived a son, you wouldn't hang around until he was old enough to marry you. Oh no, my dears, if you know what's good for you, you will go back and find new husbands. Don't stay around an old has-been like me! Anyway, God isn't against you, he's only against me.'

Orpah, distressed, kissed her mother-in-law. She felt helpless in the face of such utter desolation and began the journey back to Moab. Naomi tried to shake off Ruth too. It irked her that the girl wouldn't see reason. Why couldn't she leave her alone to wallow in her self-pity and gloom? She didn't want company in her cave of despair.

Ruth was sitting by her, holding her hand. Then she slipped down, knelt in the dust, clasped both of Naomi's hands and gazed steadily up at her. 'Do not urge me to leave you or to turn back from following you,' she entreated. 'Where you go, I will go; where you lodge, I will lodge. Your people shall be my people and your God, my God. Where you die, I will die and there will I be buried. Thus may the Lord do to me and worse if anything but death parts you and me.' Shaken, Naomi saw in those earnest brown eyes and solemn words a shining loyalty, an intense covenant love with which she could not argue.

They continued their journey. As they came near Bethlehem, some of the women came hurrying out to meet them. The welcoming smiles froze into embarrassed discomfort. Could this really be Naomi—this gaunt, grey-haired woman, head bowed and shoulders bent, looking as if she were carrying an enormous burden? Why, she seemed so old! What had happened to that once-pleasant woman? 'Welcome home, Naomi,' they said. But she snapped back at them. 'Don't call me Naomi any more. Call me Mara. God has dealt bitterly with me. He has afflicted me.'

So they retreated in dismay and left it to Ruth to conduct her to the dwelling they had prepared. 'Mara'—a 'bitter' lady! She knew she was bitter and freely admitted as much. Life had dealt her some hard blows. Enough to make anyone bitter, you might think. And yet, does it always follow that tragedy produces bitterness?

Job experienced tragedies that were calculated by Satan to leave him bitter, bewildered and cynical. What the Devil hoped to achieve was the total destruction of his trust in God, but Job refused to abandon his faith. He kept his spirit sweet. He refused to allow the pollution of bitterness to penetrate his soul. Oh, he had plenty of questions to ask, grief to express and bewilderment and anger to pour out. Yet throughout his devastating experience, he kept reminding himself of who was really in control. He did not understand the purpose, or even know if there was a purpose in it all, but he continued to believe in God's existence, his sovereignty and his goodness.

When people doubt one or all of these things, they open themselves to bitterness.

Unlike some people, Naomi did not stop believing in God, neither did she actually doubt that he was in control. She had no illusions as to his ability to prevent or allow suffering. Her problem was that she believed very definitely that he was totally responsible for her suffering and had personally inflicted it upon her. So at this stage, she did not believe in a God of love and blessing and goodness. She believed him to be cruel and vengeful.

Why? Because she based her perception of God on what happened personally to her and judged him accordingly. This is understandable in someone who has no other means by which she can determine God's character. A Christian, however, has received revelation about God—indeed, he has actually had an encounter with him. God has stepped in from outside and shown himself to be intrinsically good. His righteousness, love and mercy do not depend on what is happening on planet earth. To see him only through the spectacles of our own subjectivity—through the experiences that make up our lives—is to see a God who is too small; One who is, in fact, man-made.

If this is the only way we see him, we will collapse every time things don't happen the way we want them to. But to recognise that we are born again is to see with new eyes. It is to know a God who has invaded our darkness, confusion and despair and put within us the ability to draw on his strength in the midst of our pain.

When we are confronted with personal tragedy, God hasn't suddenly changed. He wasn't a nice daddy figure yesterday when the sun was shining and a vicious ogre today when all is cold and dark. Yet we sometimes live as if he were a capricious monster. Our security must lie in the fact: 'I am the Lord, I change not.' He is still love, light, power, joy, truth, life itself—whatever happens to us.

It is we who change—which is either good or bad, depending on how we respond to God's dealings in our lives. Naomi reacted negatively. She blamed God. She believed that he had decided to inflict agony upon her by robbing her of her main source of fulfilment.

She had a reason for saying, 'I went out full, but the Lord has brought me back empty.' The statement reveals that her fullness was her family. Now they had gone she was empty. 'Without my husband and sons,' she was saying, 'I have nothing to live for.'

So Naomi not only had a warped and limited view of God, her view of herself was affected too. She felt worthless—because her means of fulfilment had gone. She refused to see herself as 'pleasant' any more. Defiantly, she acknowledged that she was sour and bitter. So, of course, she would expect to be treated accordingly.

Wrapped up in all this somewhere was a strong sense of guilt. She believed God was punishing her for something. 'The Lord has witnessed against me and the Almighty has afflicted me. He disapproves of me; he is angry with me. He is not pleased with me.'

So the way she perceived God affected the way she looked at herself and vice versa.

Bitterness is like horrible bindweed. It looks harmless enough in its early stages of growth—just a few little pale green leaves on a slender stalk and not a thorn or a sting in sight. Yet when it begins to grow stronger, it will twist its way rapidly around an innocent planet and strangle the health out of it. Anyone who has tried to eliminate bindweed from his garden knows how formidable the task is. In my garden, I have dug up literally bucketfuls of the stringy, white roots. Yet it seems that however deep I go, I can never get them all out. When I think that there can't possibly be any left, the tiny half inch that I have missed will grow relentlessly until it is poking its incorrigible head up again. I have learned to hate bindweed with a perfect hatred! It deserves no pity and has to be dealt with ruthlessly.

FREEDOM FROM BITTERNESS

Bitterness is dangerous. It spreads and poisons. We have probably all encountered people who do not have a good word to say for anyone. They fling out barbs of criticism, attach ulterior motives to apparently good deeds and are cynical and suspicious. As unwary and gullible individuals listen to such people, they find that some of the barbs hook themselves into their own minds where they wriggle and burrow so that attitudes are spoiled and relationships affected. Well did the writer to the Hebrews warn us: 'See to it...that no root of bitterness springing up causes trouble, and by it many be defiled' (Heb 12:15).

Victims of tragedy often feel rage, frustration and pain. Their question is Why? Why? Why? They feel that their bitterness is justifiable and fuel it with large doses of self-pity. Who can blame them? And yet, indulging bitterness is so dangerous, so destructive and, once established, so hard to eliminate.

What, then, is the antidote? The clue is found in that same verse in Hebrews 12: 'See to it that no one *comes short of the grace of God*, that no root of bitterness springing up causes trouble' (italics mine). Why should the grace of God be such a key factor in dealing with bitterness?

If you are not enjoying the grace of God, you are likely to have a wrong understanding of God's character and of your own worth. Sadly, even some Christians have a distorted image of God and see him as someone who is always waiting to catch them out. To them, he is distant and hard to please. If they fail to keep the rules, he will pounce on them and make them pay for their failure. So they work hard to placate him and earn his favour. When things go wrong it is easy for them to believe that they are being punished and that God doesn't really love them. Yet they try so hard!

This sort of outlook is a nicely prepared seed bed, ready for the seeds of bitterness to take root and flourish.

But the grace of God says that he loves us unconditionally. When circumstances combine to crush us, or even when pleasant things elate us, God is not handing out punishment and reward for bad or good behaviour. His love and reliability are constant. They do not depend on our performance.

The grace of God tells us that God demonstrates his love to us in that while we were yet sinners, Christ died for us. This means that in our rebellious and sinful state God still loved us and gave his Son for us. We are accepted and forgiven. We have nothing to lose and nothing to prove. We are not trying to get into God's good books by earning his favour. He wrote our names in his book on the day we became Christians and the ink is indelible!

When we begin living in the grace of God, we will not suddenly be free from problems and pain. We will, however, have the inner ability to handle those things out of security and with a sweet spirit. We will be less likely to question his goodness and our own worth.

New Testament grace could not come to Naomi, yet she still experienced God's grace in her situation. God did not admonish her for her lack of belief, or leave her in the wilderness of depression which is where bitterness leads. Indeed, he sent a person to her who epitomised covenant love.

Ruth came from outside. She was from Moab, but she became joined to Naomi's family by marriage. When Naomi's son died, both women were widowed. Ruth was someone who could identify with Naomi. She knew what it was like to be an alien in a different land and understood the pain of bereavement. She sympathised with her weaknesses, yet did not trip into the snare of bitterness. Like our great High Priest, she drew near, fully able to empathise, yet without falling into sin.

Ruth stayed with Naomi. She refused to leave her. Again, we see the forerunner of Jesus saying, 'I will never leave you or forsake you.' Her commitment was total. She promised to stay with her mother-in-law through every remaining phase of life, even to death. She saw Naomi at her worst, lowest and darkest moments but was not deterred from her chosen path of loyalty. There must have been times when living with her mother-in-law was no joy-ride. Naomi was withdrawn, unresponsive, depressed and gloomy. Who would choose such a companion?

Perhaps there were times when Ruth was tempted to say to herself, 'Whatever did I get into this for? I could be at home where I'm known, loved and appreciated. I must be crazy!' She could have been preparing for marriage to a nice Moabite man. She could have stayed where she belonged, but she gave it all up. Why?

'For you know the grace of our Lord Jesus Christ that though he was rich, yet for your sake, he became poor, that through his poverty you might become rich' (2 Cor 8:9).

That was what was happening. Ruth had chosen to lose everything so that through the expression of covenant love—by sharing this sad woman's poverty—she might bring her through to new riches.

Her commitment was expressed in practical ways. Naomi depended on her for the very basics of life. Ruth found a job gleaning corn in the fields and became the bread-winner, yet she never robbed

Naomi of her dignity. She asked her permission before she went off to work in the fields.

Ruth's quiet, loving endurance began to produce results. When she returned from work with a big bundle of threshed corn, Naomi was roused out of her self-preoccupation to show some interest in what Ruth had been doing. She was beginning to come out of her shell, and what Ruth had to tell her fanned the faint glow within her to a flame of excitement. The man for whom Ruth had been working was not only a wealthy landowner but, more significantly, a near relative of Naomi's too. This created real possibilities in Naomi's mind for unsuspecting Ruth!

So Naomi's healing began. She took a big step when she exclaimed, 'The Lord has not withdrawn his kindness to the living and the dead.' Through Ruth's unselfish action, she was brought to see that God had not stopped being kind as she had previously supposed. In fact, amazingly, God was going to make 'all things work together for good'.

God has demonstrated his love to us by sending us a person in human flesh. He suffered with us and for us. He committed himself to us and lived a life of total unselfishness. He has shown us the value that God places upon us and the goodness of God. When we see the grace of God, we can no longer doubt his love and goodness. We can be released from bitterness.

But a big factor in release from bitterness is being able to trust in his ability to work things out for our good. This is not a passive 'what will be, will be' attitude. It is, instead, a positive belief and declaration that God can overturn Satan's strategies by reversing the effects of painful past events and making them the seed-bed for blessing instead of curse.

As Naomi uttered those words, 'The Lord has not

withdrawn his kindness,' she was contradicting her previous belief that the Lord had afflicted her. At last she was beginning to recognise that God is not capricious but steadfast.

Later, Paul wrote in the New Testament, 'Let all bitterness and wrath and anger and clamour be put away from you and be kind to one another, tender hearted, forgiving one another just as God in Christ has forgiven you' (Eph 4:32). The grace of God enables us to receive forgiveness. This also means that we can repent of our bitterness and turn away from it. Bitterness grieves the Holy Spirit because it questions God's love.

From this point, Naomi emerged from the shadows into full sunlight. Ruth had shown her unstinting care. Now it was Naomi's turn to begin caring for Ruth's destiny. Ruth carried out Naomi's instructions and the close of the book shows us a beautiful picture of the two women content and fulfilled. Ruth married Boaz and gave birth to a son, Obed.

The happy woman put the child on her lap and cared for him. The verdict of the women of Bethlehem was, 'Blessed is the Lord who has not left you without a redeemer this day.' In their eyes, Boaz was the kinsman-redeemer who had performed the expected duty of a surviving relative by marrying the dead man's widow. However, Ruth also played the part of redeemer in Naomi's life since she sacrificed her own freedom and prospects in order to liberate Naomi from her darkness. The 'riches' that Ruth left behind in no way compared with the riches that she now enjoyed and shared with Naomi.

How highly God rates covenant love! The repercussions of Ruth's action extend not only to herself and

Naomi, but spread like ripples down through the centuries. Ruth, whose name means 'friend', bore a son whose grandson became King David. It was from this royal line that Jesus, the Friend of sinners, was born. Who would have thought that such a sad, bitter woman would herself be linked with the family from which the Messiah would come?

Such is the liberating grace of God!

7
Freedom and Identity

She was ill. She had been ill for a long time—twelve years in fact. Her illness—a continual flow of blood from her body—would have drained her of energy and made her pale and weak. She would have forgotten what it was like to be fit and energetic.

She was also poor. Just as the haemorrhaging continued, so her money trickled away. Her many doctor advisers had sapped her of her finances and given her much treatment but no cure. Far from improving, her condition was actually getting worse.

She must also have felt ashamed and rejected. The Levitical law stipulated that while a woman was menstruating, she should be regarded as unclean and that anyone who touched her would be 'unclean' until evening (Lev 15:19). After twelve years of 'uncleanness', this woman must have been virtually a social outcast and a very lonely person.

In addition to her illness, poverty and isolation, she must have had an enormous struggle to keep her clothes clean and her body smelling fresh. Everything was conspiring to make her ashamed of herself, to rob her of her dignity as a person and to crush her self-image in the dust.

Maybe she had followed Jesus at a distance and had seen his healing miracles. Maybe she had said to herself, 'He's the only One who can help me, but how can I explain my problem to him when there are so many people about?' Maybe she thought, 'Why should he bother with me anyway? Nobody else does.' Whatever her negative feelings about herself, there was one overriding desire which pushed them all aside, and that was the desire to be well. It was this determination, coupled with faith in Jesus' power to heal, which prompted her to reach out and touch the edge of his cloak.

What elation she experienced following that encounter with the Lord is impossible to imagine. No longer was she a weak, pathetic sight. Jesus had completely restored her health. But more than that—he had given her back her self-respect. He had called her 'daughter'. He had commended her faith. He had approved and accepted her. He had given her peace and security. He had made her whole. She could walk away with confidence and live the rest of her life with dignity.

Although many women may not be able to identify with this woman's physical problems, they may still have a very poor self-image. If the truth were known, they suffer from acute feelings of inadequacy and inferiority. Often they are shy and afraid to advance opinions. For them, walking alone into a room full of people is sheer agony, and the prospect of facing new challenges and responsibilities fills them with fear. Sometimes they feel they would rather stay within the boundaries of what to them is familiar and 'known' rather than face the unknown. The 'known' may be unhappy, uncomfortable.

Some try to handle their feelings of worthlessness by being assertive and brash. They try to convince themselves, and everyone around them, that they are bright and confident, while all the time they are struggling inside with feeling lost and unappreciated.

External appearance can be a clue. A woman who lets herself go, who apparently doesn't care what she looks like and wears grubby, ill-assorted clothes, whose hair is unkempt and who sags drearily is saying to herself and to the world: 'Who cares? I'm not worth bothering about.' Inside she is probably aching for someone to tell her she is of value.

But it is also surprising how many smart, well-dressed women hide a low self-image beneath a trim and attractive exterior. A beautiful, glamorous woman can be convinced that she has nothing of worth to contribute to the world. In her opinion, the only good things she has are her body and face, so she works like crazy to maintain them, always dogged by the fear that she will eventually grow old and her looks will fade. 'When that happens,' she thinks to herself, 'I will have nothing left of value.' Such thoughts bring panic, so she staves them off by another aerobics class and a face-lift.

What causes a low self-image? There are many roots, but common ones are: lack of parental affection, insecurity because of a broken home, constant discouragement and comments like, 'You'll never be any good at anything!' Others feel they are academic failures or suffer because of the ridicule they experience for being different from everyone else: 'I can't stand your accent.' 'Is that your real skin colour?' 'Hi, Fatso!' Some people were simply brought up in a poor environment and were deprived of basic necessities: 'Sorry, dear, I don't have enough money to buy the clothes you want. You'll just have to make do with what you've got.' All these and many other things can cause people to feel worthless and inferior—although often the reasons are not obvious.

Is the way we see ourselves important? Or is it just a passing fad, a modern craze for self-analysis? Why not forget all that self-examination stuff and just get on with the job? Perhaps 'self-image' is a jargon expression we could do without!

It is all too easy to get diverted onto a fascinating sidetrack of amateur psychology where we are obsessed with our past; taken up with probing and poking into why we think or behave in certain ways; for ever looking for some interesting 'pimple' to press and squeeze! There is a very real danger of being seduced into endless exploration of one's psyche on the pretext of inner healing. This is simply a ploy of the Enemy to get us off the main purpose of our existence, which is to glorify God by bringing his light into a dark world. We can be for ever taking our spiritual pulses and worrying about our inward state, so that we become emotional and spiritual hypochondriacs. Our spiritual vigour becomes sapped, and our vision for the kingdom of God diminishes until it encompasses what? Just me and my needs. Instead of being an agent for bringing God's love to the world we can be constantly needing to be propped and prayed over.

But having said that, let us be clear that when the

FREEDOM AND IDENTITY

Holy Spirit brings something to our attention that needs to be dealt with, we can respond with trust. Jesus promised to send One who would guide us into all truth. If the Holy Spirit is leading the way, he will not take us down blind alleys, or get us caught up in a vortex of confusing and intriguing pictures. Rather, he will be specific in his dealings. He will bring to our consciousness the areas in our lives that he wants to change. He will expose sin so that it can be confessed and forgiven; expose hurt so that it may be healed; and expose darkness so that it can be turned to light.

The Bible says, 'As [a man] thinks within himself, so he is' (Prov 23:7). In other words, the way we think about ourselves affects our behaviour. Our self image will affect...

...our relationships

Jesus told us to love our neighbour as ourself (Lk 10:27). A man who loves his wife, loves himself (Eph 5:28). This means that if you don't love yourself very much then your neighbour or your spouse will get a raw deal!

...our expectations

Numbers 13:33 tells us that when the twelve spies returned from spying out Canaan, ten of them reported that the inhabitants were so gigantic and fearsome that 'we became like grasshoppers in our own sight'. This assessment of themselves robbed them of any expectation of victory. To them, defeat was inevitable.

...other people's expectation of us

When the time came for Samuel to anoint a king over Israel, Saul did not take his place with dignity. Rather embarrassingly, he could not be found! The people ran hither and thither looking for him and eventually he was discovered hiding among the baggage! So they ran and dragged him out. This tall, muscular man was obviously bashful and insecure. Understandably, this did not impress some men in the crowd who despised him and said, 'How can such a man deliver us?'

...our achievements

If we don't expect much of ourselves, we aim low or set no goals at all. In the parables of the talents, Jesus was not actually teaching about self-image, but the man who was given one talent behaved like a man who had a very poor view of himself. He compared himself with the one who had five and the one who had two, looked at his own single talent and decided it wasn't worth bothering about, so he buried it. Instead of viewing his one talent positively, he felt inferior and useless. In throwing away the potential that he did have, he achieved nothing.

So a low self-image can lock us up and inhibit us from entering into our God-given potential. We need a new healthy self-image.

What is a healthy self-image? There is some confusion here because some of us feel that it is right to have a humble opinion of ourselves. On the one hand, we see that Jesus was meek and lowly, a servant, and we are told we must be like him. On the other hand, we are exhorted to be in victory, to be overcomers. Then we are told that women are to be submissive, and in the next breath that they are to rise and take their place! Are humility and confidence mutually exclusive?

Paul tells us in Romans 12:3 that each of us must not think of himself more highly than he ought, but to have 'sound judgement'. It seems to me that very few women are prone to think of themselves 'too highly'. More often they have a self-image which is actually 'too lowly'. So, on what do we base 'sound judgement'?

It would have been hopeless for someone seeking to help that poor sick woman to go and exhort her to be a winner, and to stop thinking about herself. She needed specific help. She needed healing of her infirmity. But more than that, she needed someone to treat her with compassion, to give her recognition and a new sense of dignity. Fortunately, she came to the One who was able to do all these things.

How can we exchange a negative attitude towards ourselves for a positive, well-balanced one? Paul tells us in Philippians 2:5, 'Have this attitude in yourselves which was also in Christ Jesus.' Which attitude? What sort of self-image did Jesus have? That's what I need to know.

Contrary to some opinions, Jesus did not have an identity crisis. He knew without doubt who he was: equal with God, sent by God, God in the flesh. He was totally secure in his identity and therefore did not have to prove it to himself or to anyone else. The knowledge that he was the Son of God did not make him arrogant. Rather, he beautifully blended deep humility and complete confidence.

Picture Jesus at the Last Supper. There he is, welcoming his disciples, his close companions for three years. This was a special, intimate meal; his last before he was to depart from this world to go to the Father. He was fully aware of his power, identity and destiny: 'Jesus, knowing that the Father had given all things into His hands, and that He had come forth from God, and was going back to God' (Jn 13:3). What memorable speech did he then utter? What breath-taking miracle did he perform? What supernatural act accompanied that knowledge? Contrary to anything we could imagine, he took off his outer clothing, wrapped a towel round his waist and washed the disciples' feet. 'He emptied himself, taking the form of a servant...He humbled himself' (Phil 2:8).

He served out of security. Not for him the frantic service of someone desperate to be noticed; not for him the service that seems to be for others but in reality springs out of the need to be needed; not for him the attempt to win recognition in order to overcome a deep inferiority; not for him some slavish efforts to please in order to appease some sense of guilt; and certainly not for him a contrived display of 'humility' in order to impress. Jesus' service was genuine, rooted in the security of knowing who he was. That meant that his humility was genuine and his actions were unselfconscious and disinterested. They were for others, not himself.

Jesus' actions were also very deliberate. They were an example. He wanted his disciples to see that serving has a dignity of its own when it is rightly motivated. Someone who is secure and unworried about his identity has no problems with serving. He is not bothered with maintaining an image.

'Have this attitude in yourselves' (Phil 2:5). What attitude? Jesus was somebody; somebody with supreme power and authority. He had every right to be treated as a special person yet he refused to grasp it. Instead, he laid aside his specialness and became a nobody. He lived in obscurity for about thirty years, at the end of which he died, despised and rejected. By identifying with all the nobodies in history he paved the way for them to become somebodies.

FREEDOM AND IDENTITY

Our main problem is that we have believed certain negative things about ourselves for so long that our minds are set in the belief that we are still nobodies. We may have received the wonderful gospel and been set free from sin, but we can still despise ourselves and think that God despises us too.

The Enemy cannot take away our salvation, but he can try to rob us of the joy of it by whispering lies to us about our self-image. If we consistently listen to him, we shall begin to believe that what he says is true. The picture we shall then begin to adopt of ourselves will be false, or at the least distorted. What we really need to know is what God *really* thinks about us. If we can receive *his* evaluation, we will walk in truth, and the truth will set us free.

Does God think that we are miserable sinners, hopeless failures, pathetic worms? So many of us think he does. We feel that he is poised above us like a black threatening cloud, waiting for us to step over the line so that he can loose a thunderbolt on us!

The truth is that once we were hopeless captives, blind and crippled. But Jesus declared that he came to set captives free, and to open the eyes of the blind and to make cripples leap for joy! He sees us now, not as we were, but what we have become.

Perhaps my favourite picture of how God sees us women is in Psalm 45. This is a song of bubbling joy and wonder, describing the awesome majesty of the King. But who is this standing by his side? 'At Thy right hand stands the queen in gold from Ophir' (v 9). Who is this beautiful, regal figure? She can be interpreted as the church, the community of 'called-out ones', chosen by the King of kings to be his bride, his consort, the one in whom he has deposited his kingly rule. But I believe that any Christian woman can rightly see herself as a queen.

Like Queen Esther, we had nothing to commend us, but the King saw us and desired us for himself. He chose us and set his love upon us. He is not ashamed of us, but proudly declares, 'You are mine,' and has set a royal diadem upon our heads.

What is this queen doing? She stands. She is secure. She knows she has a right to be standing in the King's presence at his side. She is not embarrassed; she is not scurrying about straightening the furniture or feeling flustered about occupying such an important position; she is not afraid of being suddenly exposed as an impostor. She stands, dignified and serene, on ground that is hers, close to the King who loves her.

Where is she standing? At his right hand. This is a powerful phrase. She is not on the throne, or under the throne, or behind it or tucked away behind a curtain somewhere. She is at the King's right hand. If we look at other places in Scripture where this phrase is used, we see that it is the place of delegated authority. The 'right hand' is expected to do things! In this same Psalm we read, 'Let Thy right hand teach Thee awesome things' (v 4). Jesus occupies the throne at the right hand of the Father. It is a place of awesome responsibility as well as intimacy.

How can a woman possibly aspire to such a place? The answer is, she doesn't aspire to it, it is given to her. Our queenship is ours by virtue of our relationship to the King. It is not earned, it is not to be grasped and fought for, it is ours when we become joined to the King. That is how highly he esteems us!

What is she wearing? Royal robes. She is not playing at 'dressing up' and she hasn't borrowed them for a day to see what they feel like! They are not hired out, they don't belong to someone else—they are hers! She has the right to wear royal garments because she is who she is! She is at peace with herself. She has accepted that by virtue of being married to the King she has a new title, a new identity.

The psalmist has some emphatic advice for her: 'Listen, oh daughter, give attention and incline your ear; Forget your people and your father's house' (v 10). Why? Should she be ashamed of her past? Is there something to conceal?

David had several wives, and Solomon had hundreds. They came from different cultures, backgrounds and nations. Imagine how difficult it would be if all these foreign princesses insisted on retaining their own customs and style, or tried to impose them on others around them! They had to learn that when they married the king of Israel, they must leave their own nationality behind and adopt a new one.

One of my joys, when I have the opportunity to travel, is to meet Christian women of many nationalities. I am finding that there is a oneness that transcends our different cultures and styles. We are first and foremost not citizens of Britain or India or America or Africa, but citizens of heaven. Jesus loves us whatever our nationality—but he confers upon us a new citizenship that will last for ever. There is no room, therefore, for feeling either inferior or superior on the grounds of nationality or class or social background.

But some feel that a stigma is attached to them more specifically because of their immediate background. 'Forget...your father's house.' Some feel besmirched because of abuse, perhaps even inflicted by their fathers or a close relative. Some feel pain and guilt because of the break-up of parents, or because they were born outside of marriage and never knew a father's love or protection. But now they have been chosen by the King of kings, they come under his care and authority, they belong to a new family. The King has replaced all rags of guilt and shame with golden robes. He covers those wounds with fragrant oil and myrrh. God esteems you. See yourself through his eyes and accept his evaluation of you.

'Who am I?' How do you answer that question? We often use labels to describe ourselves. There are relationship labels: 'I'm John's wife'; 'I'm David's mother'; 'I'm Mary's sister.' Then there are occupational labels: 'I'm a teacher'; 'I'm a secretary'; 'I'm a nurse.' We have labels for different phases: child, teenager, trainee, graduate, fiancée, wife, grandma. To some degree we find security in labels and if our particular one is removed or changed we feel threatened or disorientated.

For example, women who have become used to spending most of their time at home mothering their children, can feel horribly vulnerable when their last little one goes to school. Their whole *raison d'etre* is suddenly eroded. Instead of feeling elated they can feel useless and depressed. Their security was bound up in the label 'full-time mother'. Now it has been taken away, they quickly fill the vacuum by finding another job in order to acquire another label to bolster self-esteem!

But some feel trapped by an identity that seems trivial, boring, sterile and monotonous. Perhaps the marriage is colourless, their job stifling; there is no challenge—just the prospect of endless dreariness. They see themselves as dull, unimportant and insignificant.

We need a permanent identity; one that makes us

FREEDOM AND IDENTITY

feel safe, secure and comfortable with ourselves. But it should also be elastic, not restricting, so that there is continual scope for growth and enlargement.

Can there be such an identity? One day last spring, I suddenly realised that I had found it. One of my dear friends, Poppy, who is a constant stimulus and joy to me (as she is to all who know her), came in for coffee. We were discussing our roles in life, and she suddenly asked, 'What do you see yourself as now?'

That stopped the flow for a bit while I thought about it. I thought of the various 'hats' I could wear: Terry's wife (quite a large hat since it covers a wide range of activities!), mother of five (another large and rather messy hat), speaker at women's meetings (a respectable hat?), organiser of conference days (actually, my administrator's hat doesn't fit me very well!), keep-fit enthusiast (not worn very much these days, alas), user of spiritual gifts (a halo?), author (a new, shiny hat that I'm not very comfortable with). What *am* I? Which of these 'hats' or labels is the real me?

My mind went back to a recent evening prayer meeting. It had been an exciting evening, one of a series during a week of prayer. The building was packed with people praying fervently and enthusiastically. We were ending the meeting, when suddenly one of our members came forward. 'I must share a vision with you,' he announced. He was quite stirred up and we leaned forward, expectantly.

'I could see a river, flowing from the throne of God and three words kept bubbling up out of the river. They were "success", "victory" and...' he faltered, 'I can't remember. Whatever was it?' And he punched his head with his fist. We willed him to remember. 'Come on, Doug, try.' Suddenly it came back: 'I know what it was—it was "winners"! Yes, that's it! God was saying that when we are in the river of life, we have success and victory and we are winners!'

We were elated, and applause broke out. But Doug stifled it by saying, 'Wait, God was saying something else. He was watching this river of life and all the potential that is in it for us, and then he looked at us and I felt that he was shaking his head and saying, "But oh, you English!" '

Groans and laughs broke out at this, but we got the point. In that river are all the resources for victory and success. Jesus is a winner and we are in him. But oh, we English don't really live as if we believe it. We don't have a winning mentality!

That prophecy, or vision, radically altered my outlook. Instead of being a worn out cliché, or a bit of Christian jargon, the phrase 'in Christ' came alive to me. It all made sense. I am 'in Christ', that is my address, that is my identity, my life. 'My life is hid with Christ in God.' I am in him, in that water of life. Jesus is an overcomer, he has won the victory. Whatever he initiates is fruitful. He is not into defeat, low-expectation, nil-achievement. He is into success! I am in him and his life is in me! I'm a winner because *he* is.

I turned to Poppy. 'Do you know,' I said, 'it really doesn't matter to me any more what my label is or what I call myself. I am "in Christ" and that means that whatever he tells me to do must be fruitful. It doesn't matter which of my "hats" I am currently wearing. It doesn't matter whether I am involved in something high-profile and public, like speaking at a meeting, or whether I am cooking macaroni cheese. My identity doesn't change. I am in Christ. I can be a winner whether I am praying for the sick or cleaning the sink! I'm a winner because Jesus is a winner and I am in him!'

This is so wonderfully releasing. It takes all the pressure off my striving to be someone. I don't have to struggle to define my role. I simply rest in what Christ is. All his victory is attributed to me, all his risen life is available to energise me and I haven't done a *thing* to earn it! I was born again by the grace of God and, bingo, I was in the river of life.

Stop trying to do things to find an identity. Jesus has done it all already. Just get in on his act. He's a winner and you are in him.

8

Freedom to be Whole-hearted

'It's house group tonight,' thought Sapphira. 'I'd better make sure supper's ready when Ananias comes in or we'll be late.' As she busied herself with chopping and stirring, she thought about the people in the group, and especially about the elder who was coming: Barnabas.

Everyone liked Barnabas. 'Why was that?' she wondered. Surely it was because he loved the people. He consoled them when they were down and laughed with them when they were happy. He patiently instructed them too and sometimes even gently corrected them when they needed to adjust their attitudes. Sapphira found him slightly intimidating—he could be very straight, and she wasn't used to that. She and Ananias had become adept at dodging issues and wriggling out of tight spots. Like nearly all weak, fallible human beings, they wanted to be liked and admired. This was not wrong in itself, but they had not learned that friendships and reputations are built not on showy impressions and shallow gestures but on strength of character.

What Sapphira did not recognise was the major difference between Barnabas' attitude and theirs. While he was utterly trustworthy and his words totally reliable, they got away with whatever they could. Their words were frequently questionable. Indeed, what they said was true, often turned out to be somewhat flexible.

Barnabas was a good shepherd. He looked after the lame sheep and prayed for their health. He tried to affirm Ananias and Sapphira, win their confidence and bring them into a place of safety where they could admit their needs without fear. But they lacked the courage to confront the truth about themselves. They were certainly Christians—they were saved. But instead of trusting the new river of life from within, they continued to drink from an old polluted stream. It was this stream which said to them, 'Don't totally abandon yourself to this new way of life. Who knows where it will lead? Keep your options open. Give the appearance of being whole-hearted, but keep something in reserve. Look after number one.'

Barnabas had tried hard to lead them into deeper trust in the Lord and in his word, but they never responded. The pure river of life in them was being muddied by this other stream and the fruit being produced was poisonous: lying, evasion, compromise and argumentativeness.

By and large, the church was having a glorious time. People from all walks of life were being added daily; flawed and broken individuals were receiving God's mercy and forgiveness; lives were changing;

physical healings were taking place and joy abounded. God's rule was being displayed in righteousness, peace and joy. The new believers were deepening in spiritual maturity too. Right from the start, they were receiving the apostle's teaching; they were praying and breaking bread together and working out their deep commitment to one another in daily life. Not only were they zealous to share the Good News of the gospel, they were keen to share their material possessions as well.

Most thrived in this atmosphere; but one or two, like Ananias and Sapphira, felt threatened by such close and whole-hearted fellowship. They were afraid that their secret weaknesses would be exposed, and that they would no longer be acceptable. Their fear of rejection kept them on the fringe. They knew too much to leave altogether, but were wary of being totally involved.

Many of the new Christians were fairly poor, so they did not lose much by pooling all their resources. In actual fact, they gained quite considerably. Those who were more wealthy expressed their commitment to the Lord by providing for many orphans, widows and other unfortunate people. They gave joyfully because they did not regard their possessions as things they should keep for themselves. Rather, they had 'all things in common'. It was even rumoured that Barnabas had sold a valuable plot of land and had laid the entire proceeds at the apostles' feet, trusting them to make the best use of the money.

Ananias and Sapphira were round-eyed with wonder as they digested this morsel of news. Barnabas went up another notch in their estimation. It was of particular interest to them because they too were negotiating the sale of some land. However, they felt rather under pressure now. If it became known that they had sold this land and kept all the money, they would probably be compared with Barnabas and criticised for not being as generous as he was.

Their admiration for Barnabas became mingled with irritation. They felt he had set too high an example. And yet, what a glorious gesture! It was an act for which he deserved both applause and honour, and they envied him the esteem and recognition that it brought him. How good it would be to gain that sort of respect, to be put in the same bracket as dignified, popular Barnabas!

As negotiations for the sale of the land continued, Ananias and Sapphira discussed what they should do with the money.

'We could give it all away, you know,' said Sapphira bluntly one night. 'After all, we're managing all right with our present income. If we keep it, we're likely to be taxed on it anyway.'

Ananias frowned uneasily. 'I'm not sure,' he admitted. 'We're talking about an awful lot of money. And we did inherit the plot from my mother. Is this what she would have wanted?'

Sapphira sidestepped the red herring. 'Well then, what shall we do with it?' she asked, then added some practical suggestions: 'I'd love some new clothes. We could have a good holiday and invest the rest for our grandchildren.'

This horrified Ananias. 'What would Peter and Barnabas and all the others think?' he exclaimed, ever watchful of his image. 'They'd think that was too self-indulgent for words! It wouldn't be spiritual enough! You know the Christian life is all about self-denial and taking up your cross, not about going on holiday. I'd never make house-group administrator, never mind leader!'

'Well then,' continued his wife, 'if you don't want to give it all away, or keep it all back, why not give some and keep the rest?'

But to small-minded Ananias, the answer to that was, 'It just wouldn't look so good.' He badly wanted to be esteemed and accepted like Barnabas, but he was unwilling to pay the price; to submit to the discipline required; to become a man of integrity. He wanted to have his cake and eat it—to be part of the body but to retain his independence; to follow the Lord but not to take up his cross; to have eternal life but not to die to self.

So, once again, compromise came to his aid. Yes, he would do what his wife suggested—give some and keep some. There was no harm in that. 'But there's no need to tell anyone that we kept some,' he told her. 'Let them think that we're giving the whole lot!'

Sapphira looked at him through narrowed eyes. She knew exactly what was going on in the mind of this man of hers. He was not an 'all or nothing' man. He lived on his wits, shrewd but weak, making sure there was always something to fall back on.

At this point, Ananias and Sapphira could have broken free. They could have decided to be open and honest. Was heaven holding its breath, waiting for such a change of heart? It wasn't so much what they did with the money that mattered. Indeed, they had three legitimate alternatives. They could abandon their fear, trust in a God who has promised blessings without number and gladly give it all away. They could thank God for it and, without fear of judgement, keep the whole sum. Or they could find out where the needs were greatest and openly share some of the proceeds with their brothers and sisters.

The One who owns the cattle on a thousand hills and who can turn stones into bread was not particularly concerned about the money! Of far greater concern to God were the motives of their hearts. He wanted this couple to allow themselves to be moulded like clay in the Potter's hand into the image of his Son. Would they walk out of the twilight-zone of cunning and deception and into the light? Would they, for once in their lives, honestly seek God for his will regarding the destiny of the money and then do what he said?

The Lord could never endorse a gift that was tainted by his oldest Enemy. The serpent was the source of deception. He hated radical, whole-hearted obedience. He was the father of lies who 'bent' truth and sought to warp integrity and twist righteousness. Why, the Father had sent his Son to make the crooked straight!

Oh, Ananias and Sapphira, be alert to the wiles of the Enemy! Don't defile this infant church!

Sapphira drew a deep breath and looked Ananias full in the face. 'I won't tell if you won't,' she promised.

A few weeks later, Sapphira walked confidently into the room where the church often gathered for prayer. The men had been meeting in the morning and the women planned to join them after lunch. Several paces from the door she stopped uncertainly. Something was horribly wrong.

Peter came forward and put his hand on her shoulder. Every eye was on her. 'Sapphira,' he said, 'I want to ask you a question.' She glanced at him nervously. So serious! What was going on?

'Tell me. When you and Ananias sold your land and

brought the money to the leaders, was that *all* the money you got for it?'

'They suspect,' she thought. 'But how did they guess?' Her eyes darted around the room. She swallowed and tried to control her shaking hands as her mind ran frantically through the possibilities. 'If I say, "No, we kept some," our gift won't seem so noble. We'll look mean and stingy and expose ourselves as liars. Besides, Ananias and I have agreed on our story. I can't back out now—it would be too embarrassing and he'd be furious (I wonder where he is, anyway?). No, I'd better stick to the story and bluff it out.' She tossed back her head and forced a smile. 'Yes,' she said clearly, 'that was the full price.'

Instantly, she knew she had said the wrong thing. There was an intense, suffocating silence, followed by a deep sigh from Peter. 'Why did you invent this story?' he demanded. 'Do you really think you can deliberately attempt to deceive the church and get away with it? You're not just challenging us, you're testing the Holy Spirit and he will not condone deception.'

She looked at him, dumbly, shocked into a new understanding of the seriousness of their action. In all their discussions she and Ananias had never considered that 'bending the truth' meant 'sinning against the Spirit'. Never had they thought that lying to the body of Christ was to bring dishonour to the One who proclaims, 'I am the truth.' They had simply been preoccupied about their own image and security. It had never entered their heads that the church—which was destined to be holy, righteous and undefiled—would be affected by their conduct.

She heard footsteps outside. Peter heard them too. 'They belong to the men returning from the cemetery,' he told her. 'They've buried your husband and will carry you out and bury you as well.' Instantly she dropped to the floor. When the men came in, they wound a sheet around her, carried her out and buried her next to her husband in the grave that they had dug three hours before.

The apostle Peter had declared God's judgement on lies, deception and compromise. The sceptre of righteousness is the sceptre of God's kingdom. The church must be the agent by which he establishes his government; the city set on a hill which declares his standards of living to all mankind. The church must be the light in a dark and crooked world; a lily among thorns; totally 'other'; a different species, fragrant, white and lovely.

Anything that taints the purity of the church calls into question that 'otherness'. The church is different! It is made up of those who are born again, who have put off the old nature and put on a new one. Anything that besmirches that purity provokes the question, 'To whom do you belong?' The Devil is the father of lies whose deception of Eve brought a curse on all creation. Jesus is the truth and he came to break that curse. Lies and deception cannot have any place in the church. They are characteristics of those who belong to the Enemy camp and are abhorrent.

A local church that compromises, that tolerates something so basically 'anti-God', is not a true church. It is not so much a lily as a bramble masquerading as a lily. It confuses and trips those who, thinking they have found a lily, reach out to it, only to become torn and disillusioned. The church must display the power and glory of God, bring light to the nation and demonstrate an alternative, righteous lifestyle. So it is vital for every member to be clean, whole-hearted and honest.

God has stern things to say about mixing truth and error. To the church at Laodicea, John was instructed to write, 'I know your deeds, that you are neither cold nor hot; I would that you were cold or hot. So because you are lukewarm, and neither hot nor cold, I will spit you out of My mouth' (Rev 3:15–16). Ananias and Sapphira's motives were so mixed and muddled that what could have been a commendable act became nauseating to God. God loves those who, like Barnabas, are straightforward, clear-cut, whole-hearted and free from guile.

9

Freedom to Forgive

The lady in front of me twisted her handkerchief tightly around her fingers and spoke in short, jerky, tightly-controlled sentences. Tension exuded from her.

'Tell me,' I urged.

'It's my mother,' she admitted reluctantly. 'She's old now and everyone thinks she's wonderful, but she dominates my life—even though she lives in a different town and I'm a middle-aged married woman with a life of my own. She thinks she can still order me around and expect me to run about for her. I don't know what to do,' she finished desperately.

It all flooded out. The feelings of being trapped, resentment that her life had been blighted, her efforts to please that had been constantly rejected and the wounding criticism. She was knotted up inside. How were we going to start unravelling the knot?

I knew I could not personally involve myself in this situation. I could not sort out her life, go and see her mother, or hand out advice on what to do. Thankfully, that was not what God expected of me either! But I knew I could start by helping her to face up to all the squashed, bruised feelings and bring them to the Lord Jesus. If she were to receive his help and healing, she had to be honest with herself before him.

'Jean,' I said, 'can you tell me how you feel about your mother?'

There was a short silence. 'I can't do that,' she said, avoiding my eyes.

'Why not?'

'Because it's so bad.' Then, defensively, 'I've tried and tried to forgive her.'

'You know, Jean,' I persisted gently, 'if you want Jesus to help you, you must tell him what is wrong inside. How do you feel about your mother?'

She dropped her face to her hands and tears dripped through her fingers. 'I feel so bitter. She's never let me be me. She's always dominated me.'

I put my arm around her. 'What else, Jean?' I prompted gently. 'Do you love her?'

Her head jerked up and her fists clenched. 'No!' she exclaimed vehemently. 'I know I ought to, but I hate her! Oh how I hate her!' She dropped her head again, and her body shook with sobs as she put into words what perhaps she had never articulated to anyone else before.

After a while I said, 'Jean, what would you like to say to your mother?'

Raising her tear-stained face she shook her head. 'Oh, I couldn't. It would hurt her too much!'

'But, Jean,' I reminded her, 'she isn't here now, so she won't be able to hear what you are saying. Come on now, what do you sometimes wish you could shout at her but dare not?'

Her fists clenched again, and she jerked up from the chair and shouted, 'I hate you! You always said, "Work first, play later," but it was all work and no play! You treated me like a drudge. You never loved me! I would like to make you pay for the way you walked over me and ruined my life!' She stopped, panting, a mixture of relief and shame written on her face.

'Jean, it's all right.' I said. 'God already knew what was inside you, but he wanted you to face up to it. You see, when you know what's really inside you, you can bring it to the light and let him deal with it. But all the time you are refusing to believe it's there, it's festering away in the dark. You are not giving him access to it. Let's see what the Bible says.'

I turned to Ephesians 4:31, 'Let all bitterness and wrath and anger and clamor and slander be put away from you, along with all malice.'

'Now, Jean, you have just admitted to me that inside you there is bitterness, anger, malice and hatred. Are you going to let it be put away from you? You see, it is impossible to forgive until you have been forgiven.'

Light began to dawn. 'Oh, I see,' she said reflectively. 'No wonder it didn't seem to work when I tried to forgive her. I've got all that muck to be cleared away first!'

She bowed her head and tears flowed again as she simply told the Lord Jesus that inside she felt so bitter towards her mother, so full of anger and hatred. She felt wrong about this, but didn't know what to do.

So then we looked at another scripture. The first epistle of John, chapter 1, verse 7 says: 'If we walk in the light as He Himself is in the light, we have fellowship with one another, and the blood of Jesus His Son cleanses us from all sin.'

'Jean,' I pointed out, 'Jesus is the light. In telling him how you feel you have exposed your sin and need to the light. Now it's all in the open to be dealt with. Do you want him to deal with it?'

'Yes!' she said emphatically.

Now, at this point, we may be tempted to point out indignantly that her feelings were not sin. It wasn't her fault that her mother showed her no love and understanding and made her life a misery. She was quite justified in these emotions.

But we fail to see that if we persist in this attitude, we are trying to justify what really is sin. The root of Jean's problem was not only rejection and domination by her mother—which would also need to be dealt with—but guilt about her own feelings, and it was this that we were tackling. We need to be confronted by truth if we are to be freed. That same scripture goes on: 'If we say that we have no sin, we are deceiving ourselves, and the truth is not in us' (1 Jn 1:8).

But it was my privilege to show Jean the next verse: 'If we confess our sins, He is faithful and righteous to forgive us our sins and to cleanse us from all unrighteousness' (v 9).

She then confessed to Jesus that she had been harbouring all these sinful feelings against her mother, and she asked him to forgive her and cleanse her.

'Are you forgiven?' I asked her.

'Well, if he means what he says, I am!' she replied, the first glimmer of a smile on her face.

'That's right!' I declared. 'He means it! Now let's go back to Ephesians chapter 4.'

We read again verses 31 and 32 together: 'Let all

bitterness and wrath and anger...be put away from you, along with all malice,' and affirmed that this had been done.

'Now, Jean, it says, "Be kind to one another, tender-hearted, forgiving each other." Now that you have a heart that is clean and forgiven, you can forgive, not because of your will-power or because you think you should, but because God has forgiven you. How do you feel about that?'

'I want to,' she said firmly, and prayed, 'Lord Jesus, thank you for forgiving me all my sins and especially all that I have held against my mother. Lord, out of the well of forgiveness that you have put in me, I want to forgive her. I do forgive her. I release forgiveness to her. Amen.'

I felt good about this. I know she did too. I knew that a weight of guilt had fallen off her and she felt light in her spirit. But I also knew that there was more work to be done yet. She needed to receive emotional healing for the wounds that had been inflicted on her. She needed to be released from the traumatic effects of rejection and she needed prayer to break the bondage to her mother. We had to talk about how to proceed from here in day-to-day dealings with her mother.

But the main thing was that forgiveness was the key that opened up the whole issue and made freedom possible. We underestimate the importance of forgiveness at our peril.

There are a lot of Christian people around who know that they ought to forgive because that is the Christian ethic. It is fundamental to our faith. Jesus is the great forgiver and we must be like him. But often these people feel so damaged, hurt and embittered that they can't forgive, and actually, if they are honest, they don't really want to—even though they know they should. So guilt compounds their problem. They feel alienated from God until they do forgive, but they feel he is asking altogether too much to expect them to do so!

The Enemy has a field day with people like this. Every time they resolve to forgive, he reminds them of how unfairly they have been treated, and once again they are overwhelmed by feelings of indignation and resentment. He then whispers to them that they are justified in this stance, and they become hardened in their attitude. Then he drives them further and they begin to believe that what they are feeling is righteous indignation.

But then of course they are trapped, because as soon as they try to draw near to God, there is a big heap of resentment blocking the view. Then the Enemy sidles up and piles on the guilt. 'You are not worthy to draw near to God.' So they remain poor victims, stuck fast in a huge bog of pain, hurt, bitterness and anger. As they struggle to climb out, the Enemy hurls bricks of guilt at them and they sink deeper into despair. Every time they pray the Lord's Prayer, 'Forgive as we forgive those that trespass against us,' they are confronted with their failure to forgive, and consequently are unable to receive God's forgiveness.

The incident recounted at the beginning of this chapter was obviously much abbreviated and, some might feel, rather simplistic. It is, however, the true story of how someone started out on the road to recovery. Again and again it seems to me that deeply wounded people sooner or later need to be confronted with their own need to receive forgiveness before they can forgive.

Take another example. A lady I knew was in tragic circumstances after some years of 'not-very-happy' marriage. Her husband left her for another woman and she was struggling to support herself and her children both materially and emotionally. Her world was in turmoil, but the turmoil inside her was worse.

Friends rallied around, and she received help and counsel. But one day she reached a crucial point when she was ready to begin to confront some of her feelings of anger and bitterness.

'I want to go on with God,' she told me, 'but I know I can't while I feel so badly towards my husband and the other woman. What can I do about it? I don't want to be unreal and superficial and say I forgive when I know I don't.'

'Tell me what's going on inside when you are boiling with anger at the way he has treated you,' I suggested. 'What in your heart of hearts do you want?'

Her face broke into a shame-faced grin as she admitted, 'I wish he would become impotent so that he can't have any sexual satisfaction ever again! There! Isn't that terrible?' Her frown reappeared as she asserted clearly, 'What I really want is revenge. I want him to suffer because of the way he's made me suffer.'

She went on to describe the feelings and thoughts that filled her mind as she lay alone in her bed; how she hoped that he was miserable and tortured with guilt. But indulging in these thoughts brought her no peace—they simply robbed her of sleep and made her tired and tense. 'How can I be free?' she asked desperately.

We turned to Ephesians 4 and read verses 30 to 32. 'Do not grieve the Holy Spirit.... Let all bitterness and wrath and anger and clamor and slander be put away from you, along with all malice.' I said, 'Do you see any of the emotions that you have told me about in that list?'

She was honest. 'Yes, nearly all of them, but especially bitterness and malice.'

'In the light of those verses, what do you think God feels about the situation?'

'Well,' she answered slowly, 'I suppose it grieves the Holy Spirit.'

Yes! Those things are not from God and when we harbour them and give in to them, we erect a barrier between God and ourselves. Then we are unable to receive his grace in the situation. Of course we are unable to forgive. It is at this point a Christian has a choice. She has identified her emotions and realised that they are sinful. Now, she can either bring those things into the light and let God deal with them or she can decide to stay where she is and indulge her negative emotions, feeling she is justified in doing so.

Happily, my friend was willing to humble herself. All healing and restoration starts at the cross, so she came to Jesus and told him what she felt. She said she was sorry and didn't want to feel like that any more. Would he forgive her and cleanse her?

'Now,' I said gently, 'imagine you have some big black dustbin liners. Put all the rubbish inside you into those bags. One is labelled "Anger", one "Resentment", one "Malice", and any others you want to get rid of. Now you are coming to the cross. Jesus is nailed there paying the price for all your sins. Now dump the bags at the foot of the cross. Give them to him. Can you see that they are his responsibility now? He releases you. Receive that forgiveness.'

Step by step she went through it. There was a wonderful moment when she lifted her tear-stained face and said, 'It's gone! The heavy weight inside has gone! I know I'm forgiven.'

We then went on to read verse 32: 'Be kind to one another, tender-hearted, forgiving each other, just as God in Christ also has forgiven you.'

'Now how about forgiving your husband?' I ventured. 'Instead of a pile of anger and malice inside, you now have a deep clean well of forgiveness. How about drawing some up and pouring some out for your husband and the other woman?'

She knew she could. It was no longer a problem. After that, we asked Jesus to come and start healing the emotional scars. When she left, she knew she could look to the future with an expectation of wholeness.

It is vital that we not only help people to find that key of forgiveness, and turn it, but teach them how to keep on forgiving—to cultivate a forgiving attitude. They have to learn that forgiveness is not a feeling. It is an objective truth: if I confess my sins, Jesus is faithful and will forgive and cleanse me.

So when the Enemy inevitably comes along and challenges us and tries to stir up the old feelings, we will stand on the truth. We will not fear that we won't be able to keep it up, or that tomorrow we won't feel forgiven. We will simply face him with the facts and say to him, 'Jesus has dealt with all that. I refuse to give in to indulging those feelings. I gave them to Jesus. He has paid for them; they are under his blood. If you want to know any more about them you'll have to go to him.' This takes firmness and resolution, particularly in the early days when the new shoot of forgiveness is young and tender, but as we resist him we grow firm in our faith. Each skirmish fought and won confirms us in the truth, and we develop into a seasoned warrior.

We also have to learn that we cannot afford to be thin-skinned in the Christian life. We cannot indulge in being easily offended. Some people even pride themselves on being 'sensitive'. Unfortunately, although they themselves are easily hurt or upset, they are not sensitive to the feelings of others. We all know 'touchy' people who always receive anything we say the wrong way, and we find it a constant strain relating to them because we have to choose our words so carefully when we speak to them.

Isaiah chapter 61 describes a lovely picture of broken, wounded, weak people being remade. Jesus proclaims, 'The Spirit of the Lord is upon me...to bring good news to the afflicted...to bind up the brokenhearted, to proclaim liberty to the captives.' What happens to this unpromising collection of appalling failures? They become 'oaks of righteousness'. That description says so much. An oak tree should be strong, well-rooted, majestic and full of shade-giving foliage. I like to think that a mature woman of God is like that oak tree in all these respects.

But an oak tree also has quite a thick bark and we need to be thick-skinned—in a positive way. This means that we must be secure enough to hear things said about us that could be hurtful, yet choose not to let them penetrate into our spirits. It is possible to hear something potentially hurtful, and there and then to decide if we are going to allow it to do any damage.

How do we do this? First, we recognise who is behind it. We must be alert to the wiles of the Enemy who wants to rob us of peace and bring agitation and anxiety into our lives.

Secondly, we put up our shield of faith and resist

him. We don't necessarily resist the person who has shaken us. We resist Satan's efforts to destroy our peace and stir up bitterness against that brother or sister.

Thirdly, we discern whether the hurtful remark is the truth or a lie. If it is true, we must ask God for grace to receive it. If it is not, we must remember that we are wearing the breastplate of righteousness that guards our heart. The arrow can then stick in that and be allowed to go in no further! We must not grieve the Spirit by giving way to bitterness, anger and resentment. Rather, we must maintain a forgiving attitude and keep our spirit sweet and wholesome.

Forgiveness is not a human attribute. Only the grace of God working within us enables us to forgive. Many, many people have been cruelly treated, abused and slandered, and the results are seen in physical, mental and emotional impairment. It is not rational or human to say, 'I forgive.' And yet we are commanded, 'Be kind to one another, tender-hearted, forgiving each other.'

Jesus does not demand of us more than he has endured himself. No one has received more unjust treatment than he, yet he said, 'Father, forgive them.' He has been the target of every temptation known to man and that includes the temptation to indulge in bitterness and malice, the temptation to shout, 'It isn't fair! I didn't do it! They should be hanging here, not me!' But he chose instead to forgive. Because he forgave, he makes it possible for us to forgive. But forgiveness is our choice.

Many years ago I had a very bad attitude towards a lady in the church. There wasn't any one thing that provoked me about her. I suppose we just grated on each other. Then I began to find that as I allowed my wrong feelings to continue, they affected my relationships with others, and especially my freedom to worship. I knew I had a choice before me.

One night I said to Terry, 'You go on up to bed. I need to talk to God about this.' When I was alone, I reviewed the situation. Where should I begin? For some reason I started by writing a list of all the things I didn't like about the lady. As I saw her, she was intolerant with others; she didn't listen to their viewpoint; she was obstinate and intractable, and in my ignorant and narrow-minded way of thinking, I saw her and her family as a threat to the peaceful progress of the church.

I sat back on my heels and read through the horrendous list with a self-satisfied smile. Of course I could not have a tender-hearted forgiving attitude to such an individual! Much better if she and her family all left!

What happened next totally deflated me. Almost like an audible voice I heard the words, 'What you have just written down is a picture of yourself.' I knew it was my loving Shepherd's voice—I could not doubt it. I was absolutely devastated. All my self-righteous complacency dissolved into deep conviction as I wept my way to repentance. God spoke to me again, 'Esteem others as better than yourself. Have this mind in you that was in Christ Jesus.' I realised the horrible truth that I was full of pride and arrogance and was setting myself up as a judge over my sister in Christ.

After I had received God's forgiveness, I had no trouble at all in forgiving my friend. In fact there really was nothing to forgive! Having removed the log from my own eye, I gained a more accurate perspective on the mote that was in hers!

It wasn't immediately all 'sweetness and light'. We

spent a painful evening baring our souls to each other, but we resolved to work on our relationship and to build positively. I knew that the battle was won when it occurred to me six months later that if my friend were to leave the town, it would break my heart.

The point of the story is that if we harbour an unforgiving attitude towards anyone, our vision becomes distorted. We see all the blame attached to the other person, and none to us. We become hardened in this state and then wonder why we are not enjoying the peace of God. 'Today, if you hear his voice, harden not your hearts' (Heb 3:7), or like the Israelites, you will not be able to enter into rest. Let us remain soft and tender-hearted, and cultivate a forgiving spirit.

10

Freedom and Authority

Women and Ministry

Enthusiastic applause broke out as the crown was lowered onto the new queen's head. Smiling, the king took her by the hand and led her forward to present her to his subjects.

'What's she like?' demanded a frustrated member of the crowd who, being rather short, was standing on tip-toe and craning his neck to see.

'Not bad!' was the approving comment of a more successful onlooker. 'In fact, she's absolutely gorgeous!'

'Wonder if she'll last longer than the first one, though,' was the cynical remark of another bystander. 'She was pretty too.'

'Yes, but she didn't know her place, so they say,' rejoined the short man who then added wisely, 'Wearing a crown is one thing, but knowing how to use your power is another.'

Later, as her women disrobed her and carefully removed that shining crown, Esther may well have had similar thoughts. Without her royal regalia, she was just like any other girl. 'Am I *really* a queen?' she may have wondered. 'Do I really have any authority, and if so, how far does it extend?' She may have been uneasily aware of her predecessor's fate: Queen Vashti had been deposed for attempting to assert her own will over the king's. Presumably, there were limits. Esther had better watch her step! She needed to be more than a decorative appendage to the king—she needed to fulfil her potential.

Many Christian women identify with this picture of Esther. Sooner or later we begin to realise that there is more to Christianity than simply enjoying the benefits of salvation. It is absolutely wonderful to know that we are chosen, loved and forgiven; that we live in a new dimension, with a new identity; that we have been released from an old life to experience a glorious new one. But with salvation come new responsibilities and many of us are unsure how many of these we should actually assume. What powers, if any, are rightfully ours?

Esther could have fallen into one of two traps. She could have plunged enthusiastically into fervent activity and run the risk of making the blunders associated with inexperience and naïvety. Or she could have spent most of her time on silken cushions being fanned by slaves—a passive non-achiever who took no risks at all.

In fact she took a wiser course than either of these. She adopted a humble stance, moved slowly and took opportunities as they presented themselves. She did not seek to prove her worthiness to be queen by launching into frenzied activity. She kept a low profile and stayed close to her guardian, Mordecai. When the first crisis came, it was like a preliminary test. Mordecai overheard two men plotting to murder the king and told the queen about it. Would she act or would she disclaim all responsibility? Would she say to herself: 'It's none of my business'; 'Perhaps it's not as bad as it sounds'; 'The king won't listen'; 'I'm new at this game'? No: instead, she averted the tragedy by using her influence effectively and without fuss.

Later, when faced with a crisis on a massive scale—the impending massacre of the Jewish population—she was plainly frightened but recognised her destiny and acted. She did not presume on her authority and always acted within the recognised boundaries.

As we too become aware of the authority invested in us, we must learn that there are ways laid down for us to use that power most effectively. Esther never undermined the king or questioned the validity of the accepted system of approaching him and carrying out his will. She never tried to go over his head or bulldoze him into a decision. Consequently, things got done, and she did not face premature retirement! Eventually, when the king entrusted her with the free use of his signet ring, she did not use it to further her own interests, neither did she fail to consult the new prime minister, Mordecai. She was part of a team. As she interacted with the other partners, so the effectiveness of its united government was ensured.

This mirrors the way in which the Lord Jesus himself operated. Although he knew that he was the Son of God and had unlimited power, he refused to plunge into a schedule of doing things to prove his identity. He had a brief: to set captives free, open blind eyes, heal the broken-hearted and announce the good news of the kingdom. In order to accomplish this task, he subjected himself to the authority of the Father. He did not operate independently, but claimed, 'The Son can do nothing of Himself, unless it is something He sees the Father doing' (Jn 5:19). So he carried out his brief in conjunction with the Father and under the anointing of the Spirit. They formed a team.

Similarly, all Christians must see themselves as components of a team. The powers that God gives us are to accomplish *his* will, not ours. When an ambassador is sent to work in a foreign country, he does not go as an independent individual—someone who seeks self-fulfilment and does virtually what he likes. He goes as the representative of another government and is empowered to carry out that government's orders. Enjoyment and job satisfaction are an added bonus! So it is with us.

Jesus said, 'As You [God] sent Me into the world, so I also have sent them into the world' (Jn 17:18). How was *he* sent?

He was sent *under* authority *with* authority. The Roman centurion in Matthew 8 recognised this about Jesus, 'I perceive that You are a man under authority.' Why did he say that? Since the centurion was himself a man under authority, he recognised the signs. He knew that it was like to act on behalf of a higher power. He had the weight of Rome behind him, so he could act in total confidence and security and expect results. So when his servant was cured, the centurion recognised that Jesus was working for someone else: he was an extension of heaven's authority. That's the way Jesus sends us. We are his ambassadors. We represent him and he gives us power to use on his behalf.

At this point, we probably need to clarify the distinction between two words used for 'power' in the New Testament. One is *dunamis*, from which we derive the word dynamite. It means 'force' or 'energy'. The other is *exousia*, and represents power in the sense of authority.

So the question that Christian women need to ask themselves is, 'What dynamite do we have and how are we authorised to use it?'

It seems clear to me from the Scriptures that every believer, regardless of race, sex or social status, possesses the resurrection life of Jesus (Gal 3:28). We receive this when we are born again by the Spirit of God and come alive to a new dimension—the life of the Spirit. We are offspring of Abraham, heirs of the promises of God.

On the Day of Pentecost Peter revealed a further aspect of the empowering: 'Repent, and let each of you be baptized…and you shall receive the gift of the Holy Spirit' (Acts 2:38). He made it clear that this outpouring of the Holy Spirit was for everyone: men, women and children (Acts 2:17).

All believers can therefore reckon on the life of Jesus within and receive the power of the Holy Spirit. We are exhorted to continually be 'being filled' with the Spirit. It is important for us to be constantly aware of his power and his presence.

Why is this? Because we are entrusted with a great work which we are unable to do without *dunamis* power. That great work is the bringing in and establishing of the kingdom of God. That is why we have been given the resurrection power.

How do we set about this? In what ways can we use this power?

One way is to be verbal witnesses to Jesus. Many of us shrink from this, rationalising that we are not good at it; that we lack training; that our words will be unheeded; or that we don't have the time. We feel that our efforts are doomed to failure and that our words lack punch!

If we really believed that there is power invested in the gospel and that we are authorised to use it, we would probably speak more often and with more faith. Jesus said, 'All authority has been given to Me.... Go therefore and make disciples of all nations' (Mt 28:18–19). He is all-powerful and he imparts power to us. Romans 1:16 says, 'The gospel...is the power of God for salvation.' The words that we speak so hesitantly and self-consciously are actually little hand-grenades! Let's throw a few more—not to shatter our hearers, of course, but to blast through some of the defences of the kingdom of darkness! These sort of hand-grenades can be used quite gently and still have maximum impact.

Proclaiming the gospel of the kingdom not only concerns verbal witnessing. It is not just about bringing information. It also involves power encounters with the Enemy. There are endless ways for Christian women as well as men to help alleviate the misery and suffering around us. Everywhere the evidence of a world trying to live without God screams out—suicide rates soar; marriages fall apart; and statistics rise for teenage pregnancies, alcoholism, child abuse and AIDS.

Nevertheless, God has declared that his glory will fill the earth. This will happen only as believers are mobilised to walk in the power of the Spirit, expressing the love and mercy of God—an army bringing liberation to captives, sight to the blind and hope to the despairing. Jesus' mandate has become our mandate. How can we say, 'There is nothing for women to do in the church'? We are bringing in the kingdom of God. God longs for us to stretch out our hands, to cry to him for faith, vision and power! 'The harvest is plentiful, but the labourers are few'.

This brings us to the next avenue down which to channel this power, namely, 'Therefore beseech the Lord of the harvest to send out workers into His harvest' (Mt 9:38). Prayer is an extremely effective weapon, yet we so often relegate it to 'something Christians ought to do'. Jesus taught us to pray, 'Thy kingdom come.' This is not just a nice idea or a wistful hope. It is a declaration of God's intention. It is an imperative 'Come, kingdom of God!' When we pray we should use the command militantly! We are pushing back forces of evil to make room for the increase of God's government.

Similarly, 'Thy will be done,' is not a hopeless sigh of resignation. It is a proclamation, 'Be done, will of God!' It is declaring that God has a will and a purpose. I do not have to suffer passively the attempts of the Enemy to thwart God's will in my life, or in the lives of my family or colleagues. I can lay hold of God's will, 'Lord, you have a destiny. Let your will prevail. Unleash your purposes in this situation. Let your intentions be established in this town or in this relationship.' That's powerful! That's authoritative!

Jesus has been given the name above all names and he says that we can use it for anything we want! It's like using a credit card that belongs to someone else—a millionaire! Why don't we use it more? Probably mainly because although the Spirit in us is willing, the flesh is weak—and we tend to indulge the flesh. But it may also be that we are unconvinced that our praying is a means of loosing power. We need a revelation from God about the effectiveness of fervent intercession.

Another way of utilising the dynamic within us is

through the gifts of the Spirit. God's sovereignty and man's reaching out often combine together in the Christian life. The point where they join is a mystery. We are told (1 Cor 12) that the Holy Spirit distributes the gifts among the body of Christ, but we are also urged to desire and covet them. It is as if the Holy Spirit has a warehouse full of powerful gifts which will remain there, dormant, unless we seek them. If we do not reach out the potential is wasted.

Sometimes a person may be stirred to seek, say, the gift of interpretation, and to begin to function in it. After a while, however, the novelty wears off, or they become discouraged or lazy and do not use the gift so often. Paul urges Timothy to stir up his gift—something we must be diligent to do. Let us keep a check on whether we are developing in the use of the gifts, or whether we have let them dry up.

If you want to be a blessing to the body of Christ, make sure you are using the gift(s) in which you already have some experience, and begin praying that God will enlarge your capacity for more. You will probably find that you tend to move more freely in some than in others, but all are available to you.

For example, I use the gift of tongues frequently and continually. Prophecy I also use fairly often, but from time to time I need to stir myself to do it. Prophecy (or any gift) does not come to a passive spirit! Discernment of spirits is not a gift that particularly appeals to me. I do not move in it very often, although I have asked for it in certain situations. I do, however, have friends who seem to be much more at home with this gift—they can sniff out a demon at a hundred paces!

It seems to me that I need to ask the Holy Spirit to release to me gifts that are appropriate to the occasion. I can never call them mine, but when he gives them, I can act with power and authority—his. The gifts are not for me to play with, neither are they the means whereby I can build up my prestige. They belong to God and he lets me use them to get a job done.

The word of God is also a reservoir of mighty power. Speaking out the word releases this *dunamis*. God's word is active in creation, regeneration and healing. It brings peace, joy and direction. When we declare it we are using energy which has been likened to a sword, a hammer and a great light.

So to recap: what dynamite do I have as a Christian woman? I have the same as a Christian man; that is, the life of Jesus and the power of the Holy Spirit and the word of God. They are given to me to help me live a life pleasing to God and to bring in his kingdom. This I do through the power of the gospel, the power of prayer and the gifts of the Spirit. Each of these is an umbrella which encompasses a vast number of activities, none of which is prohibited to women.

So why is the question frequently asked, 'What is there for women to do in the church?' The question implies that all doors are open to all men and virtually all shut to all women! Surely the above indicates infinite variety and scope? In fact, I would go so far as to say that there are as many things for women to do in the church as there are women to do them!

I think the question arises from a number of misconceptions. First, the false dichotomy between sacred and secular. This says there are two classes of people: clergy and laity, and in order to have a 'ministry' one has to be a member of the clergy. This is totally foreign to the New Testament. It immediately suggests the idea that some areas of service, ie those of the clergy, are more valid than those of the laity. It also suggests that there are certain acts which are more 'holy' than others. This is not true. All acts of obedience are equally acceptable—be they cleaning the car or preparing a sermon. The point is, is it what God requires of you right now?

It also creates an issue that is non-existent in the New Testament, namely, can a woman be ordained? The question is neither here nor there since the Epistles, which deal with church government, teach that all believers have an equal right to approach God. Every Christian is a priest whether man or woman. Our priesthood is not proclaimed by a special ceremony or vestments. We are priests by virtue of the blood of Jesus which gives us access to the Father (Heb 9:14; Rev 1:6).

It is therefore immaterial who administers communion. We can all minister it to one another, and in the church to which I belong, we do. Communion was never intended to be an end in itself but a means to an end. It is not some mystic ritual which has some intrinsic virtue. It is a reminder of the covenant between us and the Lord Jesus. As we remember him in his death and look forward to the ultimate reunion with him, we are refreshed and strengthened to get on with the job he has called us to do.

Secondly, the question, 'What is there for women to do in the church?' arises from a very limited view of the church. People are often under the impression that 'church' is what happens within four walls on a Sunday morning. If that is confined to a 'hymn-prayer sandwich', a fifteen-minute sermon and a handshake at the door, there is not much scope for anyone, man or woman! The only 'offices' required are an organist, a speaker and someone to open the door and lock it afterwards! Thankfully, plenty of church meetings are far more vibrant than that. We rejoice in the increasing opportunities for men and women to participate. They can pray, prophesy, bring readings, words of knowledge and prophetic songs, play an ever-greater array of musical instruments and be counsellors, stewards and teachers.

But of course, Sunday morning is the tip of the iceberg! The church is a living, breathing organism which functions twenty-four hours every day. The more it grows, the more opportunities there are to serve. We need hosts of technicians, secretaries, teachers, counsellors, administrators, drivers of vehicles, disciplers and many more. These are all works of service. As we minister to one another, we minister to the Lord.

We can get so hung up on the word 'ministry'. 'What's my ministry?' women ask themselves worriedly, and they wait for a gilt-edged label in Gothic lettering to drop out of the sky and give them instant identity and recognition. 'Ministry' is usually understood to be something fairly prominent like public speaking or healing. Many women with devoted serving hearts discount their service as too lowly to be called 'ministry'.

Ministry simply means service. We are all called to serve the Lord by serving one another. Everything the Lord commands us to do needs his power. I need his power to live righteously, to build a secure marriage and raise a family, as well as to heal the sick, cast out demons and preach the gospel.

A lady I know is training to be a beautician. She wants to help her Christian (and non-Christian) friends by being able to offer them an honest and professional service. I believe this will be a valid 'ministry' and she certainly needs the power of the Spirit as she interacts with other (less scrupulous) people in the trade. Another woman I know has a badly handicapped son. The pain and problems she and her family have suffered as a result, have opened her eyes to the helplessness of others in similar situations. She has been able to witness to many about the compassion of Jesus and is now getting involved in a handicap care programme. This is true ministry—as true and valid as that of many women in our healing teams who are used in praying for the sick and bringing deliverance to the bound.

A third reason why the question, 'What can women do in the church?' is asked, arises, I believe, from an inadequate or faulty understanding of authority *(exousia)*—and this is where we must return to our former premise that Jesus had authority, but used it under authority, and that Queen Esther is an example of this. Remember, we like they are part of a team. We are not to act independently.

Teams must have leaders. Sports teams have captains, medical teams have surgeons and consultants, business teams have supervisors and offices have managers. Is this because we like creating little dictatorships? No, it is because it is a recognised fact that if anything is going to be produced, there must be efficiency and strategy. Someone has to take the ultimate responsibility in making decisions, policies and changes. So it is not surprising that once God had set the church the task of bringing his salvation and government to the world, he decided to implement some organisation and structure.

So he gave some as apostles, some as prophets, some as evangelists, some as pastors and teachers for the express purpose of equipping—or training—the believers in their serving, and to build up, or strengthen, the whole body. We might say they are there to serve by bringing Christians into maturity and security.

Note, it says, 'he gave'. No authority in the church is up for grabs. All authority is given by God. Even Jesus said, 'All authority has been *given* to Me...' (Mt 28:18). Many men may yearn to be apostles or prophets or pastors, but if they are not the gift of God to the church, their longing is in vain. So, as regards church office, not every door stands invitingly open for 'whosoever will'!

This provokes the burning question, 'Are any leadership doors open to women?' Here we must be careful to submit first to God's word and not just to our reason or experience or emotions. As we have seen, God's power is given to women to use in many vital ways—it is not to lie dormant and unused. But we have also seen that each member of the body must work in harmony with the whole. God has given us the principles by which his power is most effectively used. If we are to exercise authority correctly, we must place ourselves under authority. Whose authority are we talking about?

First, we are under God.

Secondly (and inextricable from the first), we are under his word.

Thirdly, we are under the authority that Jesus has put in the church.

Fourthly, if we are married, we are to recognise the authority of our husbands.

Most of us have no trouble with the first two of these. It is the second two we struggle with. But if we honestly receive the first two, we must also receive the second two—since it is God's word that has given these principles.

Are these things there to limit the scope of women in the church? Assuredly not! We may have the same *dunamis* as the men, but not always the same *exousia*. A key passage here is 1 Corinthians 11, much of which is difficult to understand. What does, however, emerge clearly is that man and woman are interdependent and of equal worth. God simply wants them to observe the principle that as he is the head of Christ, so man is the head of woman. When Jesus submitted himself to the Father, he did not forfeit any of his worth or value or power. He did it to get a job done and he is my example.

In the Pastoral Epistles, Paul gives Timothy direction on recognition of elders and how they should conduct themselves. He clearly expects these to be men and teaches that women should not take authority over men (1 Tim 2:12). In the light of the body of teaching to the church, it seems that women are to be fully involved in the life of the church in every way, but that the governmental roles are to be held by the men. They are the ones who are to be responsible and accountable to God for bringing direction to the church and to individuals in it. Paul does not want women to take this sort of burden upon themselves.

As I see it, then, women should be seeking God to be fully occupied in using the *dunamis* that he has given them. They can do virtually everything that men can do in demonstrating the power of the kingdom. They can also share their experience, wisdom and knowledge in discipling and teaching. For example, women in the church to which I belong have taken seminars on inner healing, dealing with child abuse and other social issues. They have led worship, distributed communion and led women's discipleship groups. They have even, at times, attended elders' meetings and taken part in them. But they do not become elders. This would, of necessity, involve them in an authoritative and directional position in the church.

In my own church, we are fortunate enough to have elders who, rather than hold us back, actively encourage us into more. We trust them to make policy decisions, such as where to plant the next church, whether to move to another building, whether to set up a centre for AIDS victims, and who should be our next full-time youth leader (two of whom are women). They are open to hearing what others have to say, but they take the responsibility for making the decisions.

We could say that Queen Esther did not seek kingship. The fact that she remained queen did not detract from her dignity and authority. I may not be an elder, but I do not feel despised or under-rated or under-used. I trust that God's principles are the safest way both for the church to function and for me as an individual.

We can all cite examples of women in some circles who are extremely able and who are functioning as elders or pioneers. Do they not contradict this teaching? In the final analysis, I have to say that our authority is not other people's experience, but the word of God. We cannot argue from particular cases in order to establish a general rule. Thankfully, we must leave some things to God to decide, and if he appears to be endorsing a woman elder in another church, that is his prerogative—God bless her! But if we are to retain our integrity, we can only move in the light he gives us. We cannot compromise our conscience by adopting a stance we are not convinced about.

If we are talking about authority, we had better at least mention head-coverings! 'To cover or not to cover?' that is the question! At least, that is what I am often asked. I usually counter this with another question: 'What do your elders prefer you to do?'—because in the end, the Lord is more concerned with our attitude towards the authority over us than with a bit of cloth on our heads. I sometimes wonder if the Lord left this passage (1 Cor 11) deliberately unclear to test whether we would use it to demonstrate a meek spirit or a rebellious one! It is obscure, and some churches will rule that head-coverings are necessary, and some that they are not. Basically, it is all about authority and submission. Is my heart attitude right? The elders are accountable to God, so if they make a wrong decision, that is their problem! It is not a moral issue, or a matter of life or death.

Personally, I am grateful that although my elders once wanted women to wear head-coverings, they no longer require us to do so. However, even though I do not wear a hat or scarf, I feel that I need to be under their authority if I am to *have* authority. If I bring a prophecy or interpretation in a meeting, I am glad that they can weigh it, and I am helped when they endorse it. This is not repressing me, it is part of 'equipping the saints for ministry and building up the body'.

A final word regarding the authority of the husband: some husbands must learn to take authority, not just demand submission! The wives must know that their husbands are not just 'over' them, but providing support, encouragement and security as well. It is hard for a woman honestly to recognise her husband's authority if he never exerts it, if he always leaves decision-making to her and if he does not gently let her know that the buck stops with him.

I am so grateful that this is how my husband helps me. Let me end with a short illustration. Not long ago,

Terry was invited to speak at a pastors' conference in Italy and I was asked to speak to their wives. I was very torn as I weighed up the pros and cons. Several of my children seemed to need me just then and I felt that a week was a long time to be away from them at such a crucial stage. At the same time, the conference presented a wonderful opportunity to be among some lovely Italian women and I was reluctant to let it pass.

I knew that Terry felt clearly that I should go, but he wanted me to hear God for myself, so he never pushed me. This meant that I felt totally free from pressure as I prayed about it. I knew that Terry would accept it if I said 'No', because he would believe that this was how I perceived God's leading. If I said 'Yes', he would know I was going full of faith and free from guilt about leaving the children. I also had the security of knowing that if I could come to no clear decision, he would help me to make it. In the event I did go, and we are both convinced that it was the Lord's leading.

On another occasion, he noticed my downcast face as he prepared to go away yet again. That evening we discussed his absences which had become even more frequent. He took seriously what I had to say and adjusted his diary accordingly. I need never fear my husband's authority; he cares for my welfare and this makes it easy to submit to him and make room for his headship. We are a team working together. One is the leader, but both of us retain our dignity and are fulfilled.

Rather than fret about the one area that we women may not aspire to, let us profitably occupy the space that is available to us. We have all the resources that are in Christ to make the good news known in all the world. Let's intercede, let's witness, let's heal the sick and cast out demons! Let's bring love and compassion to broken people; let's serve one another with grateful hearts, working together for unity.

I don't think we'll run out of things to do or the power with which to do them!

11

Freedom and the Will of God

Submission as a way of life

The brightness faded as the angel departed. But Mary sat on in the gathering twilight, motionless, stupefied, alone with the enormity of the knowledge that she now possessed. By the time darkness had completely fallen, her pulse was nearly back to normal and her breathing was more regular. But still she remained there trying to force her numbed mind to reconstruct the details of the visit.

Only an hour ago, she had been a normal, happy, young woman, eagerly preparing for her wedding. She and her mother had spent a pleasant afternoon discussing her collection of linen. As they chatted, they smoothed and patted the sheets and hangings, admiring the quality and the delicate edging. At length, her mother had folded the last piece of material and placed it neatly on top of the pile, sighing contentedly. 'Put them away in the chest, dear,' she had said.

'I must go down and see Joseph's mother.' With that, she had gone off, leaving her daughter peacefully occupied in storing her trousseau.

When Mary's mother had left, the rays of the late afternoon sun were already spilling through the door, bathing everything in a mellow glow. Bending over the chest, Mary suddenly became aware that someone was standing in the doorway behind her. Instantly, a different, intensely white, light invaded the room. Gripped by fear, Mary turned, shielded her eyes and gazed, awestruck, as a stranger came right in and greeted her. 'Hail, honoured lady! God is with you!'

Mary, confused and trembling, sank weakly onto the chest and wondered what this greeting meant. The visitor spoke again and his voice was low and gentle. 'Don't be afraid, Mary. I've come to tell you that God has chosen to bless you in a great way.' Slightly reassured, she listened carefully as he unfolded his message.

'Very soon, you'll find out that you're going to have a baby. It will be a boy and you must call him Jesus.' The messenger began to sound very excited as he started to describe this Jesus. 'He'll be great—the Son of the Most High. He'll have David's throne—the Lord God will give it to him. He'll reign for eternity. His kingdom will never end.'

At first, Mary simply couldn't take all this in, because racing round in her mind was one fundamental question. Falteringly, she asked, 'How will this happen since I am still a virgin?'

The messenger explained, 'The Holy Spirit will come upon you—you will be overshadowed by the power of God. And the child born to you will be utterly holy—the Son of God.'

She could not see his face clearly for the brightness,

but she could not doubt that he came from God. 'He must be an angel,' she thought. There was about him an 'otherness', a purity. It did not repel or frighten her, but it did make her more intensely aware of her own humanity. As if to reassure her, the angel began to talk about her relative, Elizabeth, who, in her old age, was now six months pregnant. 'Nothing is impossible with God,' he told her.

This last statement struck a chord in Mary's heart. She knew the Scriptures. She knew that this was precisely what God had said to barren Sarah, Abraham's wife. In her old age, Sarah had borne Isaac and, miraculously, the same thing was now happening to Elizabeth. God's word was still powerful and true—and now this same word was being declared to her! But she was no barren woman, long married and forlorn in her childlessness. She was a young virgin, on the brink of marriage, with her life ahead of her!

She closed her eyes, her mind reeling with the implications. 'Will Joseph still want to marry me? And what about my parents? How can I possibly explain to them that I'm pregnant? What on earth will they say? How will they cope with the inevitable raised eyebrows, furtive glances and low whispers as friends and neighbours express their shock and outrage? Come to think of it, how will *I* face the humiliation and the embarrassment?'

The angel was waiting. He had delivered his message. Now all he needed to know was the reply. What would it be?

Did Mary have a choice? I am sure she did. Although God has already determined his purposes, he wants us to work in willing co-operation with him, not in grumbling reluctance. So he gives us choices. Remember Esther? Mordecai pointed out to her that she was in a position to rescue God's people. This was God's destiny for her, but if she did not rise to it, God would use someone else.

At first, the will of God may not appear to be a joyful thing. We may find ourselves struggling with it because it opposes our natural choice. We might want a certain job and be disappointed when someone else gets it. We might want to marry a particular guy and be heartbroken when he falls for another girl. Often we have ideas about the way ahead, but the Christian life rarely follows the path we imagine.

The will of God was tough for many people in the Bible. For Abraham, God's will apparently meant slaying his own son; for Joseph, it meant being cast into prison for a crime he never committed; for Job, it meant suffering family tragedy, sickness and rejection; for Ruth, it meant turning her back on her own country and prospects, and giving her loyalty to her bitter mother-in-law.

The most outstanding example of commitment to the will of God is seen in Jesus, who declared, 'Not My will but Thine,'—even though it meant that he had to go through the agony of the cross. Jesus shows us how to submit to God's will.

'It is my meat to do the will of him who sent me, and to accomplish his work' (Jn 4:34). The will of the Father gave Jesus complete satisfaction, pleasure, strength and purpose. He revelled in it and wanted nothing more and nothing less. His life was all about doing God's will and he looked forward to the moment when he could tell his Father: 'I have accomplished what you gave me to do,' and then sit down with no regrets.

There is a mystery surrounding the meeting point of God's pre-determined will and our decision to embrace it. I believe that the angel hovered at this point and awaited Mary's reply. God had chosen—he knew the outcome, but he was also looking for an attitude that was not passive, fatalistic or merely resigned. He was longing for the response of a heart full of joy, peace and faith; one which had positively decided to embrace his will.

We do not know how long the angel had to wait. It may have been only a few seconds, or it may have been much longer. What we do know is that the young woman eventually gave a clear, intelligent and deliberate response: 'Behold, the bond-slave of the Lord; be it done to me according to your word' (Lk 1:38).

This was no sigh of resignation. It was not, 'OK, you're the boss. I'd better fall in with your plans whether I like it or not!' In Mary's actual reply are echoes of Isaiah, who lay prostrate before the vision of God's holy might and gladly responded to God's search for a messenger, 'Here am I, send me.'

Submission to the will of God is not mere acceptance. It is not, 'Come and do this to me.' It is, instead, a positive, active laying hold of God's purposes. Paul writes vigorously, 'I will lay hold of that for which Christ laid hold of me.' He writes fervently to the Colossian Christians, 'We have not ceased to pray for you...that you may be filled with the knowledge of His will' (1:9).

Why was Paul so excited about the will of God? Why did he want above all things to lay hold of it? Why did Esther risk her life to do God's will? Why did Jesus cry out in the Garden of Gethsemane, 'Your will, not mine'? Why did Mary confidently abandon herself to the will of God, saying, 'I'm a bond-slave, let it be as you have said'?

Because they had a sense of destiny; because they

FREEDOM AND THE WILL OF GOD

knew they counted; because they could see beyond the present humiliation to the ultimate establishment of God's purposes.

That's why submission to the will of God is a glorious privilege. It is saying, 'God chose me to be part of his plan. I matter! I have a contribution. I have a destiny!' When I choose to submit to God's will, I am declaring, 'What are my puny plans in comparison with God's eternal purposes? I will gladly lay them aside for the privilege of being his woman at this time.'

When we submit to God and to his principles, power seems to be released for his will to be done. He already has a plan in mind, but he will not bulldoze it through. That's because he wants us to be co-workers with him, to share in the joys and rewards of achievement. So he waits for us to surrender our ambitions and ideas and lay hold of his. Only then can he release all the energy to put them into operation.

No wonder the Enemy hates submission! He has successfully twisted it until it has almost become a dirty word—one which smacks of repression, of being held down. Too often we have made a caricature out of what we think submission is, and then, hating that distorted interpretation, we rebel against it and reject it.

We have reduced a great and beautiful principle of the Christian life to this: 'Christian women are expected to submit to men.' As is his custom, the Enemy has perverted the truth by mixing handfuls of lies into it. He confuses the issue by subtly shifting the focus away from how we relate to the word of God and plunging us into an argument about how we relate to men. Submission is much broader than that.

Submission is at the heart of the gospel and Jesus is

our model. He submitted to the will of God in total security and peace. He laid aside the rights and privileges of kingship and embraced an alien lifestyle, suffering and death. Did he ever fear that somehow it wouldn't work; that he would be abandoned, that when it came to the crunch, he would die and never rise again? Did he fear that he would go through all the pain for nothing?

Never! We know that Jesus had complete confidence in the Father's word. This is clear from Peter's sermon on the Day of Pentecost when he attributes words from the Psalms to Jesus. 'Thou wilt not abandon my soul to hell, nor allow thy holy one to undergo decay! Thou hast made known to me the paths of life. Thou wilt make me glad with thy presence!'

Jesus knew that his submission would not be exploited. The writer to Hebrews tells us that Jesus 'for the joy set before Him endured the cross, despising the shame' (12:2). There was no fear that he would miss out, only anticipation of eternal fulfilment!

Personal abandonment to the will of God must be done in faith. We must believe that if we do what God says, he will not let us down. We must obey with the expectation of blessing, knowing that God will stand by his word. Submission to God is not a risk. We have nothing to lose and everything to gain.

So when God says, 'Give and it shall be given unto you,' we don't need to fear that we will be left penniless. And when he says, 'Be not drunk with wine, but be filled with the Holy Spirit,' we don't immediately jump to the conclusion that we shall never have any fun. And when he commands us not to have extra-marital sex, we don't suddenly think that we shall never be sexually satisfied. And if he sends us to another country for the gospel's sake, we don't anticipate that we shall live a life full of regret. And when he says, 'Wives be subject to your husbands as to the Lord,' we don't assume that we will be trodden underfoot and lose all dignity and identity. Do we?

Submission to God's will means submission to his word. We cannot have one without the other because it is in God's word that his will is revealed. The Bible gives us principles for Christian living and church government and it is only as we follow these principles that we will build a secure framework for our lives. We must make sure that we are submitted to the revealed will of God in the Scriptures before we seek from him, through events, prophecies, prayer and godly advice, the more personal and specific details of his will for our lives.

Rather than try to manipulate the Bible to fit in with our patterns of thinking, we must train our minds to adopt biblical thinking. We must not be dominated by our own ideas, humanistic philosophy, current moral values, or even traditional cultural patterns of thought; nor must we seek out some system that appeals to us and try to force the Scriptures to agree with it.

Before we could become Christians, we had to align our thinking with concepts that tend not to be palatable or acceptable to today's society. For a start, we had to admit that we needed God—an offensive thought to modern, self-sufficient people! Then we had to understand why we needed God—because we were sinners—another insult! After this, we had to realise that we were helpless to save ourselves and that the only answer to our salvation problem was through an ugly, offensive thing—the cross.

To become Christians, we therefore had to accept unpopular truths; concepts which we would naturally dislike. But when we humbled ourselves and admitted that the gospel was the truth, we found freedom. Doesn't it therefore stand to reason that just as we submitted to the word of God for salvation, we need to continue to submit to it for everything else in our Christian walk? Submission to God's word is not a mindless abdication of responsibility, nor is it a spineless passivity. We must positively embrace the word as the authority in our lives—because it is the only way to find freedom.

Jesus tells us that 'heaven and earth will pass away, but my word will never pass away'. 'The word of the Lord abides for ever.' God's whole character rests upon his word. Indeed, he *is* the Word so it is impossible to separate Jesus from it.

God cannot divorce himself from what he says. So when we come across things in the Bible that we don't like, we cannot adjust them so that they fit in with our feeble view of God. We must, indeed, adjust our thinking to fit in with the word. When we read something that makes us bristle, let's be careful before we rear up and argue, 'I don't like that bit—it can't be true.' Instead, let's remind ourselves of God's character. Does he want to put us down? Is he small-minded and petty? Is he behind the times, unable to appreciate what's happening in the twentieth century? Indeed, is he against women?

Well *is* he? You see, the issue is not: 'Are Paul and Peter against women?' If we are consistent in believing the Bible to be the revelation of God, the right questions to ask are: 'Is *God* against women? Does God want us to be repressed, unfulfilled and frustrated? Are we at a disadvantage in God's eyes?'

Have the courage to face the question head on, then see whether the rest of Scripture supports this suspicion. The resounding consensus is: God is *for* me. He has come to give me overflowing abundant life. He wants me to have joy unspeakable and full of glory. He qualifies me to share the inheritance of all his saints; to sit with him in heavenly places; to reign in life; to know his power; to use his name and to comprehend the height and depth of his love....

So where does the idea come from that the Bible is anti-women; that God wants to put us down? 'The thief comes to steal, and to kill and destroy.' It is none other than a lie of the Enemy.

How then should wives react to passages like 1 Peter chapter 3, where husbands are exhorted to 'live with your wives in an understanding way, as with a weaker vessel'? When likened to a 'weaker vessel', many women are extremely irritated and feel that Peter is being patronising and stuffy. I can't say I much like being called a 'weaker vessel' myself! Why is that? I have asked myself that question and have had to admit to having a predetermined picture of a weaker vessel which I don't like.

But 'weaker' doesn't have to mean flawed or second rate. It can refer to a difference in depth or texture, such as a 'weaker' cup of tea, or a 'weaker' shade of blue. I have had interesting discussions with men and women about the meaning of the text. What did the apostle really intend to convey? Was he simply referring to physical strength? Debatable, when one considers a woman's frequently greater resistance to sickness, or her greater fortitude in bearing severe pain—as, for example, in childbirth. Maybe he meant emotional weakness—the hormonal changes in a woman's body that can cause tension and rapid mood changes?

The temptation is to become agitated about it. But

before we do that, let's submit ourselves not to Peter, but to God whose word this really is. What, then, is God's purpose? Does he want to give men an excuse to sneer at us; to make us feel inferior? No. That is not our God!

If we look at the context of the verse, we can see that Peter is addressing husbands and urging them to take stock of their attitudes to their wives. He is exhorting the men to honour their partners, remembering that they are fellow heirs of the grace of God. It seems to me that the emphasis is not so much on the weakness, but on the strengths their wives have in Christ! To put it another way: 'You guys, don't forget, your wives are equal with you as heirs of Christ. They stand in his grace the same as you do. Now you know how they tend to put themselves down and are vulnerable to feelings of inferiority, so build them up by teaching them that their inheritance in Christ is the same as yours! Oh, and by the way, if you don't reckon to give your wife that honour, your prayers won't be answered.'

The husbands therefore need to realise that their wives have vulnerable spots, but they must not exploit them. Rather, they must encourage and stand with them. I think I can live with that! I think I have the small amount of humility required to admit that in some areas (not too many, of course!), I have weaknesses and Terry has strengths—simply because we are a man and a woman. Surely it is to my advantage not to fight against the word? After all, I do want Terry's prayers answered!

God points things out, not to hinder but to bless us. He must know better than we do—he created us in the first place. So, rather than leap to angry conclusions, it must be wiser to say, 'OK, Lord, show me

FREEDOM AND THE WILL OF GOD

where I'm weaker and where my husband is stronger, and I'll work with you on the areas where I most need your help.'

It is probably the earlier part of 1 Peter 3 that causes wives most problems. 'You wives, be submissive to your own husbands' (v 1). The chapter then exhorts them to attend more to inward character than external appearance; to cultivate 'the hidden person of the heart, with the imperishable quality of a gentle and quiet spirit' (v 4). Probably verse 6 is particularly irritating: 'Thus Sarah obeyed Abraham, calling him lord.' I may laugh at the idea of calling my husband lord, but underneath, may feel outraged: 'I'm blowed if I'm going to cringe like that before my husband.'

Hold on! We need to read on: 'You have become her children.' Do children of Abraham and Sarah do things mindlessly? No. They walk in faith (Rom 4:16). Submission to your husband is a work of faith. It is not an ego trip for the husband or a bit of doormat cringing for the wife. The key is in verse 1: 'In the same way, you wives, be submissive to your own husbands.' In what way?

This verse runs on from the previous chapter where we are reminded again of Jesus' example. As he suffered, he 'kept entrusting Himself to Him who judges righteously' (1 Pet 2:23). That is how we are to submit to our husbands—by entrusting ourselves to God who judges righteously: intelligently, deliberately and full of faith.

Some wives fear the outcome of submitting to their partners. 'He'll take advantage of me. I'll be exploited. I'll lose my identity,' they protest. Verse 6 speaks directly to them, because it says that they can be like Sarah and react 'without fear'. The word sets before us principles which we need to live out in faith—not to please men, but to please God.

The man's part is not to take advantage of his wife, but to recognise her equality in salvation, to encourage and build her up and to give her honour, consideration and recognition. The wife's part is to acknowledge him as the leader and to support and encourage him in his leadership. Together they can work out how to be fruitful for God in the light of his word.

Christian women are not told simply to submit to men. All Christians must learn to submit to one another. Submission is an attitude of mind that should prevail across the whole church. First, we must all submit to Jesus, to his will and his word. A submissive attitude should then spill over into our relationships with one another, regardless of sex, class or worldly status. Paul exhorts the Roman Christians to 'out-do one another in showing honour' (Rom 12:10). To the Philippians he writes: 'With humility of mind, let each of you regard one another as more important than himself' (Phil 2:3), and to the Ephesians: 'Be subject to one another in the fear of Christ' (Eph 5:21).

The church should be a safe place where we can listen seriously to one another's opinions, allow people to express their feelings and make use of each other's gifts. This does not mean that the church should be a democracy. There must be clear leadership, yet within and under that leadership, there needs to be an attitude of courtesy which gives dignity to each member and which remembers that God places the same value on every human soul—the blood of Christ. Submission to one another is nothing to do with playing mental gymnastics, pretending to be inferior when I know I certainly am not. It does not rest on a debased view of myself but on an elevated view of humanity.

Peter has some quite tough things to say to leaders. He tells them not to lord it over the flock, but to give themselves willingly to serving those in their charge. As they feed and care for the flock, they are serving God and exercising stewardship. The sheep entrusted to their care are precious possessions of the Great Shepherd. So if the under-shepherds are to teach them to have a submissive, serving heart, they must have one themselves.

This brings us to another area of submission: honouring the authority that God places in the church. Jesus is the head of the church, so if we build to his blueprint, we will be safe. In his wisdom, Jesus has decided to delegate authority for running his church. These men: apostles, prophets, evangelists, pastors and teachers, are his gifts to us (Eph 4), so we should not regard them with suspicion or fear. Their specific purpose is the 'equipping of the saints for the work of service, to the building up of the body of Christ' (v 13). One day they will be unnecessary—when we finally come to 'the measure of the stature which belongs to the fulness of Christ'.

In the meantime, men and women are called to honour the leaders who 'diligently labor among you, and have charge over you in the Lord and give you instruction,' and see that 'you esteem them very highly in love because of their work' (1 Thess 5:12–13). If these men know that they are accountable to God and are therefore walking humbly before him and others, and if they are caring diligently and compassionately for us, then we have nothing to fear from submitting to them. A good shepherd is there to bring us into security and maturity. He protects and promotes, he defines limits and opens doors, he encourages us to rest, but he also motivates us to move on. In other words, he offers a safe environment in which we can grow up and develop the gifts that God has given to us.

I am so thankful that I enjoy the loving protection of my elders. In fact, I recently asked for their protection to be increased! For several years I have organised 'Leading Ladies' Days' for leaders' wives and other women with responsibility in several different churches. These days are primarily to give the women help, teaching and fellowship.

However, a couple of years ago, I began to feel uneasy and vulnerable. I had as much scope as I could handle. I could arrange a day, send out letters and speak to the women—and no one was checking up on me! Although I knew that there were women present who would not hesitate to pull me into line as necessary, I still did not feel entirely safe. I sensed that I needed the endorsement and covering of the eldership.

So it was arranged that if I was involved in any important meetings or activities, I would discuss them beforehand with two of my elders. I now share with them my thoughts about the theme of any meeting that I am taking. They can correct me if necessary, and I am reassured by their approval of what I am going to say. As a result, I am able to speak with greater, not less, confidence and clarity. I want to be instrumental in establishing a healthy church and believe that my submission to God's delegated authority is a means to that end.

There are the occasional horror stories where authority has been abused. Sadly, it is these infrequent

FREEDOM AND THE WILL OF GOD

occurrences which tend to get publicised and cause people to fear submission to leadership in case they too get wounded.

Where there is an eldership problem, there is also a clear procedure for dealing with it. Paul warns us, 'Do not receive an accusation against an elder except on the basis of two or three witnesses. Those who continue in sin, rebuke in the presence of all, so that the rest also may be fearful of sinning' (1 Tim 5:19–20).

We must not be quick to judge an elder, but if there are several witnesses to his sin, then his leadership must be questioned. And if he continues in sin, he must be publicly rebuked. The fear of God must rule in the situation. Eldership is a great responsibility and that's why Paul warns Timothy not to be in too much of a hurry to bring elders to office. The answer to 'abused authority' is not 'no authority', it is 'righteous authority'.

Lastly, the church is also instructed to be subject to the civil governing authorities. 'There is no authority except from God' (Rom 13:1). This raises all sorts of ethical questions like, 'What about Godless regimes?' and, 'What about atheistic governments?' Paul, who lived under a Roman Emperor, knew all about this, but both he and Peter agree on the issue. We must not compromise our faith, and when there is a point of conflict our first allegiance is to King Jesus. However, we must 'as far as possible live at peace with all men'.

The word of God tells us to adopt an attitude of mind which positively and deliberately places itself under the rules and laws of the land. Unless there is something which our Christian consciences refuse to allow us to do, we should do our utmost to uphold these laws. Let's do as Paul directs—respect the government and pray for it.

We so prize our independence and individualism that we fear submission will make us mindless and irresponsible. We want to stick up for our rights, have our own way, make our mark. But this is a human way of thinking which makes no provision for God.

We must not allow ourselves to be conformed to this world, but to have our minds changed. God can do nothing with us if we are stiff-necked and proud. 'God is opposed to the proud, but gives grace to the humble' (Jas 4:6). Are you afraid of the doormat syndrome? What will happen to you if you bow to the Scriptures; to the will of God; to your fellow Christians; your elders or your husband? Are you afraid that you will be steam-rollered and crushed into becoming a narrow-minded, boring robot, without an original thought in your head?

Mary was confronted with a plan which would change the course of her life, bring her pain and discomfort, and cause embarrassment to her family. Did she regret her answer of whole-hearted submission: 'Behold, the bond-slave of the Lord; be it done to me according to your word' (Lk 1:38)?

In the magnificent outpouring of worship enshrined in what has come to be known as the 'Magnificat', we catch a glimpse of a spirit that is freed from the anchors of self-interest. It soars in joy with the privilege of being harnessed into the mighty purposes of God. This is not the voice of a passive, narrow mind, crushed into fearful obedience.

The repercussions of her submission affect every generation and, amazingly, even our eternal destiny. No one will ever be asked again to do what she did, but we are all called to lay down our own wills in favour of God's plan. Jesus taught us to pray daily, 'Be done, will of God!'

The choice to submit to God's will may often seem hard and perplexing. Like Mary, we may find ourselves asking, 'How can this be?' The answer is the same: 'The Holy Spirit will come upon you,' and that holy thing which will be brought to birth in you is the will of God.

Many years later, when her Son was fully grown and moving into his ministry, some men came to Mary with a problem. Her advice was this: 'Whatever He says to you, do it.'

12

Using Truth to Fight for Freedom

We straggled up the path from the beach—a bunch of tired people looking forward to their supper. On a warm, sunny day the beach would have been a great place to be, but on a grey, drizzly day, with a chill wind blowing in from the Atlantic, a beach in Brittany was too bleak for comfort. So as the wind roared across the sand, making our food gritty and our skin goose-fleshed and bluish, we had given up the struggle to relax. Instead, we had collected our buckets, spades, towels, children and other paraphernalia and were now on our way up to the campsite.

Perhaps I was disappointed with the weather, or maybe it was the awareness that what awaited us was not an inviting, snug home but a flapping tent; not a warm supper all ready but the prospect of a rather unimaginative meal taken from packets and cooked on camping equipment. Whatever it was, I was not in a cheerful, forbearing mood. So when we eventually arrived at the tent and discovered that four-year-old Simon had lost one of his shoes, I felt very annoyed indeed. He had only brought one pair and could hardly be expected to continue the rest of his holiday in France with only one shoe!

'We must have left it on the beach,' said Terry. I sighed. 'It certainly looks that way,' I agreed, 'but we've got to find it! Blow, blow, blow!' We searched around for a while, my frustration mounting. Eventually I blurted out, 'Well, one of us has got to go back to the beach and look for it. It might as well be me!' So off I trotted, retracing our steps down the rocky path, under a cloud of martyrdom, irritation and self-pity.

I wasn't aware of what was happening at first. As I jogged along I was thinking, 'This is such a nuisance—and just when I should be preparing supper! Of course, it's always *me* who volunteers for acts of unselfishness. I'm the one who is always ready to help, who will go the extra mile, who is uncomplaining and humble! It's typical of me to rush to volunteer to run all this way on my own! Why didn't Terry volunteer? Why didn't he immediately offer to go? Why does he always leave all the nasty bits to me?'

And so the unsavoury monologue went on, and I, blind and stupid in my pride, did not perceive that another unseen presence was running along beside me, pouring all this garbage into my willing ears. Every thought he flung into my mind I eagerly received, believed and swallowed until tears of self-pity were stinging my eyes—only I did not call it self-pity. If challenged, I would have called it 'justifiable indignation' or 'righteous anger'. How we love to dignify our petty, peevish behaviour with long words!

By the time I reached the beach I was really worked

up. Suddenly, I had an objective glimpse of myself. I had actually reached weeping point, and through my mind flashed the question: 'Why are you crying?'

I stopped. Why *was* I crying? I didn't know! Puzzled, I stood still and wondered, 'Why am I acting as if I'm the victim of some injustice? Why do I feel cross and sulky and hurt? Nobody has forced me to do this. It was my idea, my decision to come back to the beach.'

Suddenly, all became clear. Like sunlight breaking through cloud, revelation came to me. My mind and my emotions were being battered from the outside. As I had run down the cliff path, the Enemy, or one of his agents, had been running alongside, busily flinging fiery darts into my susceptible mind. I had not been on the alert. I had not recognised him. I had received his lies about Terry and myself and swallowed them whole, and now here I was reduced to a pathetic, snivelling heap!

Standing on a rock on a beach in Brittany, I understood. I had the freedom to make a choice. I could choose to continue to wallow in what I now clearly identified as self-pity. I could look for the shoe—all the time feeding my thoughts of self-righteousness—and return to the camp with an air of martyrdom. I could act 'hurt' and be cool and distant. In other words, I could be completely passive, allowing sin to have dominion over me. I had that choice. Or I could take my stand there and then and resist the Enemy. I had that right and that authority.

I stood still on that rock and faced my taunter. 'I resist you, Satan!' I shouted. 'I stand in the grace of God! I submit to him, not you! How dare you come at me with your filthy lies! I tell you it is not my will to

USING TRUTH TO FIGHT FOR FREEDOM 153

indulge in self-pity any longer. I will not have it. Get off my back! Be gone!'

The wind took my words and they were lost in the sound of the waves and in the cries of the seagulls. But I knew they were heard. 'Submit therefore to God. Resist the devil and he will flee from you' (Jas 4:7). There was, however, more to do yet. The sword of the Spirit had quenched my assailant's attack, and I didn't need to be preoccupied with him, but I had to arm myself against his return. 'Resist him, firm in your faith' (1 Pet 5:9).

How do we do that? We have to know who we are and on what ground we stand. We gird ourselves with truth and guard our minds with the helmet of salvation. We put up the shield of righteousness which protects our hearts from Satan's accusing, condemning blows. I should have done it before, but it was not too late.

Still standing on that rock (what a good thing the beach was deserted!), I declared, 'I am a child of the living God. I am redeemed, forgiven. I am born again. Satan, you cannot take this ground from me. I stand upon what Jesus has done. I do not resist you by myself—I am in Christ!'

Cheered and emboldened, I began to skip from rock to rock, singing and shouting praise to the Lord, mingling my English with other tongues. Joy surged up within me. I was free!

I did not find the shoe. We located it under a bush near the tent the next morning. But my encounter on the beach taught me a lesson which I have never forgotten. It was a small skirmish and only took a few minutes, but I had discovered a principle which works whenever the Enemy attacks. I have used it frequently: in my kitchen, in the car and in meetings. It is always effective. Sometimes the combat lasts much longer, but I am confident in the authority of the word of God and I know that will always win.

Really, it's all there in the word: 'Submit therefore to God.' That simply means: 'Let God's light shine on you, exposing your weakness. Come down off your high horse; humble yourself. What you are indulging in is sin. Call a spade a spade.'

Having recognised that, you then have a choice: to continue in sin, or to resist the Enemy. 'Resist the devil and he will flee from you.' He has to recognise a higher authority.

How do you resist? 'Firm in your faith.' You must know who you are and where you stand, and you must arm yourself with truth and keep fighting.

Then 'draw near to God and He will draw near to you' (Jas 4:8). He comes close and encourages and supports you. He is delighted that his victory makes you victorious.

The trouble is that we live so carelessly, so unaware of what is really happening. The Bible tells us to 'be on the alert, for your adversary, the devil, prowls about like a roaring lion, seeking someone to devour' (1 Pet 5:8). We drift along happily and let our defences slip. Suddenly, the Enemy throws a banana skin in our path—we are assailed by jealousy, or lust, or anger. We skid helplessly and crash down, and there we sit blaming our friends, or our circumstances, or even God, for what has happened to us. We feel guilty, condemned, a failure, and it takes a major rescue operation to get us on our feet again.

Be on the alert! And when a fiery dart does come whistling towards you don't stand there waiting to be struck! Get the shield up and the sword out. The truth will make you free.

13

The Vision of Freedom

I saw the sign 'Public Footpath' and pulled the car into the side of the road. I climbed over the gate and set out on the path that skirted a field. The grass was long and thick. Away to my right the Downs shimmered in the afternoon sun. Clumps of trees on the bare slopes made rounded woolly shapes. Above, the sky was streaked with high white cloud and the wind made the long grass bend and swish around me like green waves.

The Sussex countryside had never looked lovelier. I revelled in its prolific foliage, the tangles of brambles and cow-parsley, the smells and sounds and colours of high summer. There is no sweeter place on earth than an English hedgerow at the foot of the Downs on a drowsy afternoon in late July. So why did I feel a low, dull ache inside? I had been grappling with it for a few days. Now I knew I must take it out and expose it to the merciful gaze of the Lord.

I reached the corner of the field and found a small gate, obviously little used, and tugged it free of the overflowing brambles. On the other side I found myself at a point where another field opened on my right, golden with corn. But somehow I felt drawn to a narrow little path that led on ahead and I plunged into the thick undergrowth. The path was only just discernible, apparently unfrequented by humans but with evidences of the recent presence of cows!

I felt faintly annoyed as I became hemmed in by trees each side, which cut out the light and the view of the Downs. That was where I really wanted to be—up there in the sunlight, unhindered by nettles and bushes, where I could run and feel the wind. Yet somehow I knew I had to go this way.

There *was* a path. It was small, winding and uninviting. I couldn't see where it was going. 'Never mind,' I said to myself, 'it can only get better. It must open out soon.' At one point a bird, startled by the unusual intrusion of my presence, fluttered out almost under my feet and perched precariously on a low bramble. It was a very young thrush, its tail feathers not yet fully grown. Frozen with fright, it waited on the twig while I stretched out my hand. I almost had it in my grasp when it recovered its senses and fluttered away in a frenzy. My hand brushed its wing.

Then before me the path entered what appeared to be a tunnel where trees darkly overhung and the ground trodden by many hooves was muddy and wet. Pools of stagnant water lay here and there. It was a dank and fetid place. I looked at it and shrank from it. I tossed up in my mind—should I turn back or continue? After all, I was taking an afternoon walk. No one was forcing me to go this way! And my new red trainers would get soiled! But still an inner urge nudged me on.

It looked so bad, but I found islands of solid ground that supported my weight, and so I pressed on. Eventually I crossed the boggy forbidding place and came onto relatively dry ground. The trees fell back and the path wound on through the mass of undergrowth. Soon I came to another gate where I stopped.

On the other side was a quiet grassy meadow, full of clover and drowsing bees. At the end of it I glimpsed a home, pleasantly situated, a picture of peace and contentment. I stood and looked and pondered; and I said to the Lord, as I had said many times during this short walk: 'Lord, what are you saying to me?'

I felt his presence. Psalm 23 rose up in my mind and as I turned round to retrace my footsteps down the overgrowing track, through the dark, muddy section again and on to where the tracks crossed, I found myself repeating it again and again. 'The Lord is my shepherd.' He has promised to lead me and guide me. The path won't always be pretty but his protection, direction, nourishment and presence are promised to me. I thought about how I had sought him for guidance for the seminars I was taking at the Downs Bible Week, and how I had been led to explore the theme of freedom. I had prepared and spoken in the knowledge that if that was what God wanted the women to hear, it must be because many were not experiencing freedom in many areas of their lives. And so it had proved. Many areas of bondage had surfaced, and I and other helpers had prayed with many to be set free. But it was frustrating to realise that often during these sessions we had only uncovered the tip of an iceberg. Many of those seeking release needed prolonged help and careful nurturing and discipling. As many as possible were instructed to go back to elders and leaders at home and work through these things in their local church community.

But some came from churches which lacked skilled counsellors or the necessary caring structures, and some had come alone, not yet attached to a church. Still others were at a very vulnerable stage and felt it difficult to divulge their needs to people who knew them well. I had been unprepared for the grief I felt rising in my own soul as I heard story after sad story of abuse, neglect, rejection, failure and sorrow. I had begun to question if I should ever have got into this whole realm. I did not feel that my primary mission in life was to inner healing. I didn't like it; I felt ignorant, unqualified and was afraid of messing up people even more.

But that afternoon the Lord showed me again that part of preaching the gospel and teaching his word is dealing with the repercussions that emerge. This may not be my main path in life, but it was a track that he would lead me down from time to time—a path through people's lives, tangled emotions, choked up with despair and cares, even through the shadowy valleys where demons lurked—but all with a view to bringing them to the open sunlight of God's love and presence with the prospect of safety, warmth and security.

Back on my walk I came out to the open space where the paths met and was drawn to the field of standing corn. I hung over the gate, enraptured by the sight before me. The field was vast, the corn was so brightly golden, so tall, so ripe. The sight of such abundance took my breath away.

I went through the gate and sat down. The sun was

high and hot. I shut my eyes and all I could hear was the wind rustling that vast golden sea of ripe corn. 'The field is the world.' I wept. 'O God!' I cried again, 'what are you saying?' He seemed to say, 'It's harvest time. The harvest will be abundant.'

The thought of the millions who need freedom can be oppressive; but the vision of that golden harvest before us can inspire and motivate us to share the freedom we have found. We can have a part in gathering it in. We can be co-labourers with him in setting captives free.

Leading Ladies
Women of the Bible speak to leaders' wives today

by Wendy Virgo

Adam—Moses—David—Samson—Job

—each had a wife who either supported his life and ministry, or contributed to its downfall. Queen Esther had her own unique role. What can we learn from these and other leading ladies of the past?

Wendy Virgo skilfully retells and examines the biblical stories, to show leaders' wives today how they can fulfil their roles in a high-pressure world. Whether you are married to an itinerant preacher or a youth-group leader, you will find principles to help develop a ministry that both supports and complements that of your husband.

> *Wendy has sought to display the biblical picture of a woman not crushed into mindless submission but released into fulfilling ministry through honest observance of the biblical safeguards.*
> Terry Virgo

Wendy Virgo is respected for her ministry to leaders' wives in many churches. She is married to well-known church leader Terry Virgo, and they have five children.

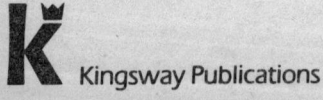